"Re-Engineering" Dual Training – The Malaysian Experience

T0326514

Berufliche Bildung in Forschung, Schule und Arbeitswelt

Vocational Education and Training: Research and Practice

Herausgegeben von Falk Howe und Georg Spöttl

Band 1

PETER LANG

Frankfurt am Main · Berlin · Bern · Bruxelles · New York · Oxford · Wien

Gert Loose/Georg Spöttl/Yusoff Md. Sahir (eds.)

"Re-Engineering" Dual Training – The Malaysian Experience

PETER LANG
Internationaler Verlag der Wissenschaften

Bibliographic Information published by the Deutsche Nationalbibliothek
The Deutsche Nationalbibliothek lists this publication in the Deutsche Nationalbibliografie; detailed bibliographic data is available in the internet at <http://www.d-nb.de>.

ISSN 1865-844X
ISBN 978-3-631-57722-6

© Peter Lang GmbH
Internationaler Verlag der Wissenschaften
Frankfurt am Main 2008
All rights reserved.

Printed in Germany 1 2 3 4 6 7

www.peterlang.de

The essence of effective training lies first of all in the *determination and engagement of the private sector* to provide quality training and in the *self-directed commitment of the trainees* to exploit this resource.

This publication is dedicated to *Datuk Muhammad Feisol bin Haji Hassan* who has been relentless in conveying his inspiration and in his vigorous support for the implementation of highly effective training in Malaysia and to the late *Horst Lemke (†)* to whom we owe the subtle, practical understanding of the essence of effective training.

Printed with the generous support of Deutsche Gesellschaft für Technische Zusammenarbeit (GTZ) GmbH and the German Malaysian Institute (GMI)

gtz   **GMI**

History of the Publication and Acknowledgements

This publication originated from an international conference held on the occasion of the 10th anniversary of the German-Malaysian Institute (GMI) at the Renaissance Hotel in Kuala Lumpur in 2003. In line with GMI's main concern in training the theme of the Conference was *Employer-Based Training*. Very special thanks go to Abd. Rahim Jusoh who has superbly prepared the complete scenario for all presentations at the conference including the necessary pre-sessions with the speakers. He was in all this work intensely assisted by Raja Aziz.

However, what had over years under Dr. Abdul Hakim Juri, the first Managing Director of GMI been developed as "training close to industry" became under GMI's second Managing Director Yusoff Md. Sahir more and more the basis for the conceptual development of a learning approach for dual training. These developments were in particular followed by Ngan Cheng Hwa, the head of GMI's human resource department.

From 2000 to 2005 GTZ's Dual System Project-team: Gert Loose, Hermann Koch, Wolfram Pforte, Stefan Erber and others worked in a close and very successful symbiosis under the Human Resource Section in the Economic Development Unit of the Prime Minister's Department. Raja Dato Zaharaton binti Raja Zainal Abidin, Datin Faizah Mohd. Tahir and Othman Mustapha inspired and guided the first phase of the project's development later on followed by Datin Halipah Binti Esa, Dr. Wan Abdul Aziz Wan Abdullah, and Zanifa Mohd. Zain. Over all these years GMI's development staff was the project's highly valued partner.

After the Dual System Project came to a close, Yusoff Md. Sahir, Hermann Koch and Ngan Cheng Hwa continued this work together. At the same time core development tasks on the operational level were taken over by the Human Resource Development Council (MLVK), today's Department of Skill Development in the Ministry of Human Resources. With this endeavour a number of talented and committed young development staff joined this work. They were guided most of all by Wan Seman bin Ahmed, Pang Chau Leong and Ghalip Spahat.

In a new phase of GMI's development work, training programmes were offered for dual training teachers, instructors and coaches in industry. Furthermore instructional quality was upgraded by conveying Learn and Work Assignments (LWAs) as an integrated innovative approach for promoting self-directed learning. This work has been developed to high standards by Mazlina Ahmed, Raihan Tahir, Nabilah Ooi Abdullah, Hasmawati Ismail, Suhaila Hani Zaini and Yusfamarhaini Mohd Yusoff.

For the superb logistics behind all these developments our special gratitude goes to Abrar Baharuddin and Munah Osman and many others who rendered help and friendly advise.

Finally Graham Attwell and Regina Spöttl have brilliantly edited the collection of diverse papers and Marc Timm has perfected the layout in his usual professional way. Marc Timm and Torsten Grantz provided help with the work on the paper and supported the authors especially in editing the figures and Sadiq Al Muscati has been so kind to do the proofreading for the whole manuscript.

Table of Contents

Excerpt from a Letter by the Former Secretary-General to the President of the UN General Assembly [A/56/422, 28 September 2001]

Kofi A. Annan, Former Secretary-General of the United Nations

Excerpt from a Letter by the Secretary-General to the President of UN General Assembly (A/56/422, 28 September 2001)

"In my report to the Millennium Assembly of the United Nations, I called the attention of the world leaders to the urgency of addressing the problem of unemployment and underemployment of young people.

I furthermore committed myself to convening, together with the heads of the World Bank and the International Labour Organization, a high-level policy network on youth employment drawing on the most creative leaders in private industry, civil society and economic policy to explore imaginative approaches to this difficult challenge. Heads of State and Government meeting at the Millennium Summit took up this challenge when, in the Millennium Declaration, they resolved to develop and implement strategies that give young people everywhere a real chance to find decent and productive work."

Preface

This publication has emerged from the analysis of issues which focus on effective training in an international perspective and from the desire of the Malaysian Government to secure world class training for its workforce. Yet, before we open the discussion regarding the valid parameters which govern effective training we would like to highlight the most pressing need faced by many young people in developing countries: their fruitless longing for *any kind* of decent and productive work. We are therefore convinced that whatever our achievements in designing effective training may be, we must be aware of and sympathetic to the pressing need for creating basic opportunities for work. In support of this insight, the former Secretary-General of the United Nations, Kofi A. Annan has called upon the Heads of State and Government to develop and implement strategies that would give young people everywhere a real chance to find decent and productive work. We would like to join this call and to endorse it with a quotation at the beginning of this publication.

Compared with the desperate situation created by the deplorable absence of work opportunities, it is surely a privilege to elaborate on ways of achieving the most effective preparation for skilled work. And in fact despite the worldwide need for strategies which secure decent and productive work for everybody, we are seeing impressive economic development in Southeast Asia and other parts of the world, leading to attractive employment opportunities. Lean production lines and efficient transportation logistics have assisted these countries in creating global markets for their products. Yet, beyond production and distribution, these fast developing countries have also become interlinked through effective training systems which help stimulate the economy. Undeniably, designing the most efficient means of providing the skills for the national high-tech workforce has become a central concern in particular for the ambitious economies in South-East-Asia.

Excellence in high-tech work must be based on excellence in training. Training based on targeting specific competencies – commonly known as "competency-based training" – was seen as a way to achieve this excellence. However, this apparently logical approach, which seemed to make it the panacea for meeting today's pressing high-tech training needs, has failed to keep its promise. Yet, its undisputable contribution to the development of highly effective training has been to create awareness that the necessary accountability of training can only be secured through the definition of occupational standards. However, when they only reflect the immediate *work* which has to be carried out at the workplace, occupational standards seemingly fall short. The rapidly changing context of work also needs to be reflected, and therefore a new focus on the *work process* is needed to guide the necessary reorientation in training.

Ironically, the "dual" training system of the countries in Central Europe had almost been discarded as inflexible, too restrictive for youth and too demanding on employers. However, the full impact of rapid technological change and increasing complexity at the workplace created a high degree of uncertainty regarding the specific skills needed. Modes of training based on competencies could no longer cope with this uncertainty, and in this dilemma the "dual" mode of training, with its vital component of on-site training at the workplace, was found to be better capable of encompassing the dynamics of the work process. Therefore the trend in development has swung back to the dual system approach, with countries such as Australia opening rapidly growing programmes in this field.

So in the midst of all these developments, we ask: What have we learnt to help us better design high-tech training? The basis for efficient training is now increasingly seen as being what we have always known: *training is preparation for performance at the workplace*. And we have further elaborated this simple insight into the basis for operation in training. With constant massive change and uncertainty at the *workplace* it has become indispensable: our main scenario for training must be right there; we must persist with "hanging in" with the process of change where it happens *at the workplace*. Any approaches which rely on analysing and documenting the actual skill requirements away from the workplace itself are in no way suitable to grasp the ongoing dynamic change which is characteristic for modern work life.

Only through a structured work-process analysis has it become possible to access the potential experience at the workplace and present it in the form of occupational standards for knowledge workers (k-workers). These are displayed in the form of the *core work processes* of a given training occupation which outline the generic skills which comprise it. Hence, we are able today to define *occupational standards* which reflect the actual skill requirements of the modern, constantly changing workplace with a closeness and precision which was wanting before.

Next to the mode of training – and partly even overlapping with it – the main concern of this publication is with the availability of the *appropriate learning environments* for effective training. Ambitious national training programmes consume huge resources for up-to-date facilities and advanced equipment in training institutions. And yet the return on these investments is questionable. Rapid technological change renders expensive equipment outdated within a couple of years. Hence barely used sophisticated machinery may already prove to be useless, but the replacement is likely to be too expensive to be ordered right away. Public *budgets for high-tech training equipment cannot keep pace* with the advances in technology.

And even where appropriate technology is available in the training institution its simulated use may be far away from the parameters of actual application at the workplace. In particular most *sociopsychological and interpersonal dimensions of work cannot be simulated*. And finally, employment policies – at least in public-sector training institutions – tend to favour long-term employment of teaching personnel. Therefore there is a considerable risk that tenured training personnel may have been hired along with equipment which is no longer in use at the actual workplace; and their skills consequently may no longer represent the actual needs; yet they continue to pass them on to their trainees.

The definitive answer to these problems can only be to promote training at the actual workplace. This mode of *practical training* which is supported in a balanced way by sufficient *theoretical instruction* is commonly called "dual training". This refers to the coordinated use of the two learning environments, the *workplace* and the *classroom*. Austria, Switzerland and Germany have long-standing experience in this field. Other industrialized countries such as Australia (see Andy Smith's article in this publication) have exerted tremendous efforts to create their own version of this mode of training.

Finally, this all brings us back to the question which is crucial for establishing quality training: Can we achieve a real, consensual cooperation with the private sector in conducting training? Our conceptual brilliance and devotion to investments in training will be in vain, if we do not manage to conduct together with the private sector the kind of training which is truly needed in the workplace. Interestingly, recent experience clearly demonstrates that developing occupational standards through a *work-process analysis* is not only a tool for designing training. It can at the same time be a powerful strategy for opening the doors of industry and *developing a true partnership in training*. Too often when representatives of industry and public training meet to cooperate the result is controversy and misunderstanding because of differing expectations on both sides. Yet, when the representatives of the two sides meet at the workplace to conduct together a work-process analysis the mutual efforts for designing an appropriate blueprint for effective training tend to pave the way for a lasting cooperation. Occupational standards which have been developed and implemented jointly have proven to be a secure pathway to a smart partnership between training institutions and the private sector.

Regarding the implementation of these insights in national training systems, Central Europe still seems to be standing aside, mostly confined to following the historical traits of "dual" training, while *Malaysia* has taken the initiative to carefully design and define her own approach to training. The emerging Malaysian National Dual Training System (NDTS) has to be regarded as unique in *combining the accountability of competency-based training with the exploitation of the richness of on-site practical experience of the "dual" mode of training*. It represents Malaysia's attempt to learn from best practice in training all over the world, yet, to finally create a truly Malaysian system of training.

This publication reflects the analysis of best practice in training which centers around the workplace in lead countries as well as the philosophy, policies and procedures of the emerging Malaysian National Dual Training System. With this broad scope in mind the articles in this publication attempt to present a case study for "The Re-Engineering of Dual Training: The Malaysian Experience."

They look at the concept of a work-process orientation in training, the experience of an "old" (Germany) and a "new" (Australia) dual training country, the important role of the global players in generating global competence, advanced learning strategies in high-tech training, and finally, a synopsis of all the aspects which form the basis for the introduction of the National Dual Training System in Malaysia. Government policies, the analysis of private sector needs and the elaboration of national strategies for human resource development all are essential elements of the baseline for an emerging dual training system in Malaysia.

Gert Loose   Georg Spöttl   Yusoff Md. Sahir

Muscat   **Bremen**   **Kuala Lumpur**

Chapter 1: Network to Support Youth Employment

Education and employment are stressed by the former Secretary-General of the United Nations as two closely related types of opportunities. The Youth Employment Network (YEN) – a network which is supported by the World Bank and the International Labour Organisation (ILO) at the highest political level – shall safeguard that governments, civil societies, and economic politics take up these issues in order to guarantee that education and employment are pursued in a way to safeguard youth employment. The article not only underlines the high significance of this concern but also the importance for securing appropriate work for young people.

It is being reported that high-level members of the network have prepared a set of policy recommendations in order to endow the international community with an important impetus and to mobilize political commitment and practical action to swiftly increase employment opportunities for the youth.

As recommended by a high-ranking panel, the Secretary-General encouraged the Member States to draw up national action plans on youth employment as a matter of priority. He also invited the International Labour Organisation to take the lead in supporting the implementation of the panel's recommendations. And finally he has requested the panel to continue to act in an advisory capacity on the issue of youth employment.

A New Partnership to Prepare Young People for the Knowledge Economy: The Secretary-General's Youth Employment Network

Steven K. Miller

The following chapter will focus on presenting the UN Secretary-General's Youth Employment Network including its political dimensions, some of the policy orientations that underpin this Network, and their implications for active labour market policies of countries at different levels of development.

More than 1 billion people today are between 15 and 25 years of age and nearly 40 per cent of the world's population are below the age of 20. However, eighty-five per cent of young people live in developing countries where the vast majority of them are struggling to learn and work in a context of extreme poverty. According to World Bank figures, approximately 1.2 billion people struggle for survival on per capita incomes of less than US $ 1 per day (Lim/ Miller 1998). Throughout the world, young people are two to three times more likely to find themselves unemployed when compared to adults. Kofi Annan, in his report to the Millennium Summit of the United Nations, writes that demography is not destiny and that "if I had one wish for the new millennium, it would be that we treat this challenge as an opportunity for all, not a lottery in which most of us will lose."

Within these statistics as our backdrop, what are the political dimensions of the Secretary-General's Youth Employment Network? You may recall that in September 2000 the largest gathering of Heads of State and Government ever met at the United Nations in New York at what was called the Millennium Summit. In preparation for this meeting, Kofi Annan issued a special report entitled "We the Peoples: the Role of the United Nations in the Twenty-first Century". In this report, the Secretary-General presented a host of new initiatives organized under four topics: globalization and governance, freedom from want, freedom from fear, sustaining our future and renewing the United Nations. Generating opportunities for the young was presented as a means to achieve freedom from want. Generating digital bridges through information and communication technologies, a theme highly relevant to youth employment, also figures prominently in his report. And when referring to "opportunities" for the young, the Secretary-General stressed two closely related types of opportunity: education and employment. It is also in this report where the Secretary-General first proposed his Youth Employment Network in the following terms (Annan 2000):

> "Together with the heads of the World Bank and the International Labour Organization, I am convening a high-level policy network on youth employment drawing on the most creative leaders in private industry, civil society and economic policy to explore imaginative approaches to this difficult challenge. I will ask this policy network to propose a set of recommendations that I can convey to world leaders within a year. The possible sources of solutions will include the internet and the informal sector, especially the contribution that small enterprises can make to employment generation."

The Secretary-General's statement underlines the importance and urgency of addressing youth employment, but furthermore is an admission that we in the United Nations do not yet have the answers on how to create the necessary jobs. Therefore he appointed a panel of 12 experts from around the world and from different backgrounds, not only to come up with policy recommendations on youth employment, but also to launch a political process and concrete action in this field.

Although the Youth Employment Network is an initiative of the Secretary-General, it draws on a strong political mandate from United Nations member states. As part of the Millennium Declaration, the final outcome of the Millennium Summit, Heads of State and Government universally agreed to "develop and implement strategies that give young people everywhere a real chance to find decent and productive work."[1]

Based on this mandate, both from the Secretary-General and from the United Nations' General Assembly, preparations began for what turned out to be an informal but extremely productive first meeting of the high-level panel of the Youth Employment Network. Thematic working groups were set up, and preparatory meetings held, which explored the following five dimensions of the youth employment challenge:

- Information and communications technologies,
- Vocational education and training,
- The informal economy,
- The role of the employment in national poverty reduction strategies,
- The youth employment dimension of development strategies.

Based on the results of these thematic working groups, organized under the leadership of the ILO, the World Bank and the United Nations Division for Social Policy and Development, the Secretariat prepared an issues paper and a first draft of policy recommendations for consideration of the high-level panel. This twelve-member panel, together with James Wolfensohn, the President of the World Bank, Juan Somavia, Director-General of the International Labour Organization, and under the chairmanship of Kofi Annan, then met for the first time at ILO Headquarters last July.

At this meeting, Mr. Kofi Annan emphasized the need for both immediate action and long-term commitment to achieving the millennium goal on youth employment. He also invited the panel to continue working with Mr. Wolfensohn, Mr. Somavia and himself in an advisory capacity on an ongoing basis as a standing panel. Finally, he requested the ILO to take the lead in organizing the future work of the YEN and to assume the responsibility for hosting a permanent secretariat.

Following this meeting, the panel has finalized its policy recommendations, which include an ambitious process designed to hold political leaders to their word. The panel's recommendations encourage world leaders to translate their commitment made at the Millennium Summit into action through a specific political process. First, Heads of State and Government are invited to develop national action plans with targets for the

---

1   General Assembly resolution 55/2, para. 20.

creation of jobs and for the reduction of unemployment, and to take personal responsibility for presenting these plans to the United Nations. The preparation of these actions plans should be based on a critical review of past national policies. A willingness to learn from more successful countries is another element for consideration.

Ten governments are invited to volunteer to be champions of this process, to take the lead in preparing their action plans and in showing the way to others. In developing their plans, governments are encouraged to closely involve young people and to adopt an integrated concept for employment policy. Employment policy is seen not a sectoral policy among others, but rather as the successful mobilization of all public policies.

The ILO is then invited to prepare a global review and evaluation of these action plans and report back to the General Assembly to provide a basis for longer-term political processes. Let me now draw a few implications and conclusions from the political process that I have just described.

First, youth employment provides an entry point into broader, and thornier, employment policy issues. Youth employment is an issue on which political consensus can be easily developed. Developing solid strategies for youth employment provides a first step for political leaders and policy makers in addressing tougher issues of creating employment for all groups within society where there may be difficult trade-offs to face.

Second, the political commitment of governments provides a space for action for a variety of non-governmental actors, including employers, trade unions and organizations of young people themselves. Therefore, the political process of preparing national action plans is not an objective in itself but rather a means to encourage public-private partnerships in developing concrete action for youth employment.

Third, this political process allows the United Nations, the World Bank and specialized agencies of the United Nations system such as the International Labour Organization to work together with member states and their constituents in new ways.

Now let's take a look at the high-level panel's policy recommendations on youth employment.

The recommendations begin by presenting youth as an asset, not as a problem. This is an important political message, particularly in the wake of recent events which tend to present young people as an enormous problem, or more euphemistically, as "challenge" to be addressed. An article appearing in the New York Times "Week in Review" quotes stunning figures to say (Sciolino 2001):

> "From Casablanca to Kabul, the statistics are stunning. Well over half the populations of Egypt, Syria, Saudi Arabia, Iran, and Iraq are under 25 years old. In Pakistan, the number is 61 per cent; in Afghanistan, 62 per cent. The boom in young people coming of age in a broad swath of territory where terrorists recruit might seem to pose one of the United States' most daunting national security threats."

However, rather than focusing on young people as potential terrorists or threats, the Secretary-General's panel chooses to focus on the positive and creative potential of young people:

"Young people are an asset in building a better world today, not a problem. In the next 10 years 1.2 billion young women and men will enter into the working age population, the best educated and trained generation of young people ever, a great potential for economic and social development."

Also, the panel presents youth as a creative force today not only tomorrow. In other words, it avoids speaking of young people as "tomorrow's leaders, but rather speaks of them as today's partners:

"Young people are now asking that their voices be heard, that issues affecting them be addressed and that their roles be recognized. Rather than being viewed as a target group for which employment must be found, they want to be accepted as partners for development, helping to chart a common course and shaping the future for everyone."

Secondly, while the panel was concerned with delivering a technically anchored message, first and foremost, it wanted to deliver a political message – a simple, understandable message intended to influence policy makers. If active labour market policies in favour of youth employment are to be successful, they must operate at both at political and technically operational levels.

This message can be summarized in four Es:

- Employability: invest in education and vocational training for young people, and improve the impact of those investments;

- Equal opportunities: give young women the same opportunities as young men;

- Entrepreneurship: make it easier to start and run enterprises to provide more and better jobs for young women and men;

- Employment creation: place employment creation at the centre of the macro-economic policy.

We will now touch briefly on each of these four points and analyze the implications they have for countries at different levels of development.

First, *employability*. The panel calls for breaking the vicious circle of poor education and training, poor jobs and poverty. All countries need to review, rethink and reorient their education, vocational training and labour market policies to facilitate the school to work transition and to give young people – particularly those who are disadvantaged because of disabilities or who face discrimination because of race, religion or ethnicity – a head-start in working life. Each country is invited to set objectives and targets based on best practice/best performance for investment in education and training and other employability strengthening measures, leading to jobs and social justice for the young.

For young people to be employable, the prerequisites are literacy, basic education and then training, all of which must be relevant to industry and labour market needs. Hence, employability opens the door to issues of education and training which are particularly important in creating good quality employment or "decent work." By upgrading the employability and skills of the work force, education and training stimulates a race to the top rather than a race to the bottom. Rather than the natural trade off between the quantity and quality of employment, training links both these factors in a virtuous circle of more and better jobs for young people.

At this point it may be useful to discuss the implications for employability in developing countries. Typically, in industrialized countries, one associates high levels of education with low levels of youth unemployment. However, there is an apparent anomaly in many developing countries where high levels of formal education, particularly secondary and higher education, may be associated with high levels of unemployment as well as with high levels of frustration amongst these unemployed youth. Educated youth in developing countries tend to come from better off sections of the population and have correspondingly high levels of expectations.

As stated in a recent ILO Report, in many developing countries "only the better educated can afford to be unemployed" (International Labour Office 1999, p. 7). Whereas in most industrialized countries that make up the OECD there appears a strong correlation between education, employment and decent work, in most developing countries unemployment rates for the more educated exceed those of the less educated. Therefore the challenge is to better utilize the precious resource of growing numbers of educated young people in the developing world – a resource which is being wasted at great cost to young people and to society at large. The other side of the coin is the challenge of upgrading the employment opportunities of those without adequate education and training working in dead-end jobs in the informal economy (e.g. International Labour Office 2001, 2004, 2005).

Low income young people do not have access to the same educational opportunities and cannot afford to forgo immediate income earning opportunities in order to invest in education. Therefore a vast majority of young people in the developing world turn to employment in the informal economy to eke out a living. The challenge for young people working in this sector is not to make them employable, but rather to upgrade the productivity, incomes and levels of social protection of the employment on which they depend.

At the 2002 International Labour Conference of the ILO, the informal economy was a subject for discussion. Twenty-years ago, when the ILO first discussed this issue, there was a sentiment that the informal sector was a transitory phenomenon, which would gradually disappear as development took place. However, at present, not only is employment in the informal economy on the rise, but through international sub-contracting and outsourcing arrangements the boundaries between formal and informal economies are becoming increasingly blurred. A strategy to upgrade youth employment in the informal economy needs to be carefully designed to exploit positive and discourage negative linkages between the two economies. Sub-contracting and outsourcing are being increasingly utilized as a means to sidestep fundamental labour standards. Increasing attention should be paid to bring informal sector enterprises under the protection of fundamental principles and rights at work. This requires a combination of strong and enabling public policies in order to avoid a situation where vulnerable small enterprises, including home workers and other forms of self-employment, are forced into a race to the bottom to ensure their access to wider markets.

As for the educated and frustrated young people in developing countries, the trick is not just to re-orient public education and training policies away from expectations of employment in the public sector, but also to implement public policies which stimulate employment growth in the private sector. For many developing countries, this means implementing policies targeted at the creation of a vibrant, employment-intensive and productivity-enhancing domestic private sector.

As much as youth employment is a concern of all countries at all levels of development, it is particularly a concern in developing countries where the vast majority of today's youth live and work. In most developing countries (which lack public and in-stitutionalized forms of social protection) the only safety nets for the unemployed are those of familial and informal networks. For most young people in developing countries open unemployment is a luxury they can ill afford. They therefore turn to the informal economy for survival. More work is needed to upgrade the basic education and skills of workers in the informal economy and to develop training delivery systems adapted to the needs of these workers. Here the key is not to create new jobs in the informal sector, but rather to improve the quality of those jobs that exist already. Education and training policies and delivery systems must be adapted to be effective for working in this growing informal economy.

The word "employability" has been at times criticized for implying that if job seekers are unemployed this situation is their own fault. However, as taken by the panel, this term combines both the responsibility of the individual and that of the society. The individual is responsible for taking initiative and seeking out new opportunities. However, the society is responsible for providing these opportunities through an environment in which discrimination is not allowed to become an obstacle to an individual's employability – hence the reference to social justice in the context of employability.

This recommendation takes a stand in favour of the high road to employment, what the ILO Director-General refers to as not just any job, but rather "decent work." This type of employment, which requires a young person to be well educated and endowed with skills relevant to the labour market, produces a young person who will be looking for better quality work. Employability is also closely linked to information and commu-nication technologies through making these more widely available and accessible, and to closing the digital divide.

The message of employability is a message of not just individual responsibility, but also one of social justice, of the right of young people to education and training which will lead them to decent work and to the type of society where race, religion, ethnicity or disabilities do not get in the way of employment.

Equal opportunities for young women and men: The panel provides two sets of arguments to underpin this recommendation. One is based on a moral imperative, and the other as a means to boost productivity. The recommendation reads: "Eliminating the gender gap in educational, training and job opportunities is not only a moral imperative, but furthermore, a means to increase productivity and quality of employment". In many countries, where boys and girls have equal access to education, girls are achieving more than boys in school. In a great many countries girls are not getting the same education opportunities as boys with serious gender gaps in literacy as a consequence. The panel argues that all countries need to review, rethink and reorient their policies to ensure that there are equal opportunities for young women when they enter the workforce and throughout their working lives. Each country should set objectives and targets to rectify the gender disparities in access to education, training and labour markets, and develop and implement the necessary gender sensitive policies in these areas.

Entrepreneurship: Entrepreneurship is not just about self-employment and helping young people start their own business. Neither is it merely about encouraging the private sector to create employment. Certainly, these are key pieces of the puzzle. But in calling for strengthened entrepreneurship, the panel is calling for a renewed sense of initiative for all young people, be they workers or employers, working in the private or in the public sector.

Hernando de Soto, one of the panel members, makes a strong plea to review many cumbersome regulations which keep the poor from starting their own business. While entrepreneurship is not for everyone, it is a means of creating new employment opportunities for both workers and for employers. All countries need to review, rethink and reorient the legal and institutional framework for business to make it easier to start and run a business. Governments and international organizations should make it a top priority to obtain real, reliable and relevant data on the informal economy and on the rules and procedures required to set up and operate a new business within a legal framework. Based on a better understanding of the institutional obstacles, policies should be developed to allow this part of the economic system to be integrated into the mainstream economy and raise its productivity through legal facilitation. This review should be combined with respect for labour standards that should be seen as a basic element in achieving productivity and prosperity.

Governments, on national and local level, need to encourage a broad and dynamic concept of entrepreneurship to stimulate both personal initiative and initiatives in a broad variety of organizations that include, but reach beyond, the private sector; small and large enterprises, social entrepreneurs, cooperatives, and the public sector; the trade union movement and youth organizations. Countries also need to strengthen policies and programmes so that small enterprises can flourish and create decent work within an enabling environment.   Each country should set objectives and targets for a broad reform programme based on best practice that will offer more flexibility for enterprises and more security for workers.

Employment creation: A cross-country analysis of youth employment carried out by the ILO in 1997 (O'Higgins 1997) concluded that general macroeconomic conditions have overwhelming influence in determining the level of youth employment. However, youth unemployment is more sensitive than adult unemployment to changes in aggregate demand. This is one of the reasons that, overall, youth unemployment rates tend to be two to three times higher than the rates of adult unemployment. One of the many reasons why youth are disproportionately affected by changes in macroeconomic conditions relates to levels of acquired training. The costs to firms of firing young people is lower than for older workers since they represent lower levels of acquired skills and human capital.

While youth are hurt more than adults by economic downturns, macroeconomic policies, which stimulate aggregate demand, also carry the potential of benefiting youth disproportionately. In fact, the fourth "E," employment creation, underpins all the three other "Es", namely employability, equal opportunities and entrepreneurship. Employability requires not just appropriate skills and training, but also public policies that lead to new employment opportunities where these skills can be used. Investing in youth requires not only better skilled youth, but also a commitment by public and private sector partners to keep job creation as a central concern of their investment strategies. Equality should follow a high road leading to increased opportunities for both women and men. And entrepreneurship should be supported not only through structural measures, but also through growth-oriented macro-economic policies so that enterprises can sustain themselves.

I shall conclude with an example demonstrating an enormous opportunity to create new sources of employment for young people in developing countries which is particularly relevant to the work of the World Bank, and indeed, the broader international development community. Infrastructure investments represent a missed opportunity where the potential for employment creation is greatly under-estimated and under-exploited. The World Bank estimated in the 1994 World Development Report that, at that time, developing countries invested US $ 200 billion a year in new infrastructure – 4 percent of their national output and a fifth of their total investment. In preparation for the UN International Conference on Financing for Development, the World Bank appealed for major, immediate infrastructure investments to address the urgent needs of poorest segments of the population facing "infrastructure poverty." However, for such infrastructure to effectively reduce poverty, greater attention needs to be paid to the employment potential of such infrastructure investments.

Utilizing cost-effective labour-intensive methods for the construction and maintenance of basic infrastructure is one means of getting an employment bonus for young people out of infrastructure investments. Small-scale basic infrastructure of direct benefit to the poor, such as agricultural feeder roads, low-income urban upgrading schemes, irrigation and water supply, soil conservation and environmental restoration works are all of immediate benefit to the poor, and furthermore lend themselves to labour-intensive methods. Also, the workforce in labour-intensive infrastructure development programmes tends to be made up of a large proportion of young people.

The World Bank and the ILO have collaborated in this field for a number of years. Experience has shown that labour-intensive public works can be implemented with timely and high quality results. Also, such "public" works can be implemented by the private sector, and provide one opportunity for young people to start viable enterprises, in small-scale contracting, in engineering consulting and in a variety of ancillary services.

References

Annan, K. A. (2000). *We the Peoples: The Role of the United Nations in the Twenty-first Century.* United Nations.

Garonna, P.; Reboani, P.; & Sziraczki, G. (2000). *Achieving Transparency in Skills Markets: Measurement and Information Gaps in Education and Training Statistics.* Franco Angeli, Milan.

International Labour Office (1999). *Employing Youth: Promoting Employment-Intensive Growth,* ILO, Geneva.

International Labour Office (2001). *Youth and Work: Global Trends.* Geneva.

International Labour Office (2004). *Improving Prospects For Young Women And Men In The World Of Work: A Guide To Youth Employment.* Geneva.

International Labour Office (2005). *Youth: Pathway to Decent Work.* Geneva.

Lim, H; Miller, S. (1998). *The Future of Urban Employment.* International Labour Office, Geneva.

O'Higgins, N. (1997). *The Challenge of Youth Employment.* Employment and Training Paper No. 7, International Labour Office, Geneva.

O'Higgins, N. (1997). *The Challenge of Youth Unemployment.* ILO Employment and Training Papers No. 7, International Labour Office, Geneva, 1997.

O'Higgins, N. (2001). *Youth Unemployment and Employment Politics: A global Perspective.* International Labour Office, Geneva.

Sciolino, E. (2001). Radicalism: *Is the Devil in the Demography?* New York Times Week in Review, December 9, 2001.

United Nations. *Letter from the Secretary-General*, Document A/56/422.

Chapter 2: Learning with Close Links to the World of Work – A Success Story?

It is the inescapable truth that we *remember just 10 per cent of what we have seen, yet, we remember 90 per cent of what we have done* (Kowalczik; Ottich. Schülern auf die Sprünge helfen. rororo, 1998.). With this basic insight in mind it is no longer a surprise that training at the workplace has to be regarded as the most effective mode of conveying the skills which are needed for successful performance at work.

The tremendous change which we are witnessing today at the workplace can only be countered through arranging the training right there in the work process. Our trainees today need to learn in the work process to be prepared *for* the work process. The unfolding of this dual role of the work process as the site for training as well as for work is explained in the first article of this chapter.

However, the impact of modern technology and the increasing complexity of the objects of work have made it mandatory today in most occupations to master substantial background knowledge as a pre-requisite of effective work. Therefore, learning practical skills at the workplace has to be matched by learning the necessary related theory. This requires the classroom as a second learning environment.

Training which relies on a combination of utilizing the workplace and the classroom as the two learning environments is commonly referred to as apprenticeship or the "dual system of training". Worldwide this mode of training has been implemented in different variations. The experience of two countries with a strong tradition of effective training, Germany and Australia are presented here.

And finally the dual system of training and competency-based education and training are often seen as competitive modes of preparation for employment. A discussion note further investigates the common ground of understanding needed in order to render these two modes really comparable.

Learning through the Work Process – Challenges and the Shaping of Skill Requirements

Georg Spöttl

Preface

Learning at the workplace is increasingly assuming importance both in practice and in public discussion. Small enterprises cherish the hope that much of the new knowledge and skills required for coping with modern work tasks may be acquired "as-you-go". They deliberately or unknowingly presume that learning by working is a unorganised, non-supported way of learning. However, according to research, learning during working hours is considered equally important as a self-organised and supported form of learning through the work process[1]. Functional and intentional learning is clearly differentiated when it comes to learning at the workplace (cf. Livingstone, 1999, p. 65 et seq.). This is a first step towards achieving the slogan of the "learning enterprise".

Staudts and Kriegesmann, in their publication "Mythos Weiterbildung" (1999), show the limitations of traditional course or seminar based training[2]. They report the following reasons to explain the lack of attendance at training courses:

- 50 % of the interviewees cited a lack of time,

- 40 % felt that the courses took place at inconvenient times,

- 40 % indicated family duties,

- One third complained that the courses were too expensive (cf. Livingstone, 1999, p. 76).

Learning at the workplace has the decisive advantage that learning is done alongside working. Special seminars, the provision of teachers, teaching rooms and learning infrastructure are rendered obsolete. Nevertheless, it must be admitted that our scientific knowledge of the learning processes involved in learning during the work process is still limited (cf. Mora et al., 1999, p.3).

---

1   Above all in vocational training and adult education a variety of methods and a connection between learning and work were called for and also put into practice to a much greater extent than in the school context. At least in large and medium-sized companies, training times at the workplaces have been increased and integrated into forms of work and learning. Quality circles etc. were created.

2   Staudt and a number of American surveys point out that just 10 % of all seminars qualify their participants for a better accomplishment of their jobs. In the United States this figure equals a loss of about 90 Billions of US $.

The Importance of Learning at the Workplace in Enterprises

Learning at the workplace implies that work and the work environment are organised in a way that the workers themselves may solve problems, albeit with support. Companies must trust their employees and provide a work environment which not only permits but also promotes learning. This calls for an integration of work and learning. The organisational structures in a company have to be designed in a way to create the necessary spaces for learning to take place. Another approach is to shape work processes in order to link them with the development of competencies. When these minimum requirements are met, there is an increased opportunity for employees to acquire new knowledge and competencies through the work process. Once such developments are initiated in a company, it is possible for the workforce to advance alongside changes in work demands. The challenges of new technologies can be more easily and more speedily resolved. Technologies may be applied in order to integrate learning and work. However, technology and work organisation have to be shaped in a way that makes learning and working feasible. There will be a continuous development process for employees and the company which enables both parties to cope with new work tasks and to safeguard the future (cf. Spöttl 2004 p.186; Butt 2005).

The Development of Competencies through Learning at the Workplace

Learning at the workplace is usually combined with the idea to develop competencies by coping with work processes. Developing competencies has become a crucial issue for developing a workforce that can achieve competitive success. "The increasingly important issue of developing competency in order to create a smart workforce leads to a further demand for efficient ways to manage training and development in organisations" (Sandberg, 2000, p. 48; Spöttl 2002). However, in order to manage training, managers need to understand what constitutes human competence at work.

The development of competence raises questions such as:

- What can be learned at the workplace?
- What pre-requisites are necessary for a workplace learning environment?
- What is the quality of workplace learning?

To date, there are few empirical studies available in this field (cf. Stegmaier, 2000). Dreyfus and Dreyfus (2000) investigated the acquisition of competency among aeroplane pilots, chess players etc.

> "A central finding from their study was that attributes used in accomplishing work are primarily not context-free but are rather linked to a particular type of work situation, regardless of the level of competency acquisition. Results demonstrated that as soon as workers begin acquiring experience in a particular type of work they start to acquire knowledge and skills that are not context-free but, on the contrary, are situational or context-dependent" (Sandberg, 2000, p. 51).

These findings are backed by recent research that underlines the importance of context-related knowledge and suggests that context orientation is a crucial pre-requisite for an increased competency in problem solving (Gerstenmaier, 1999, p. 66). This finding questions the significance of key qualifications.

A number of studies of workplace practice pointed out that the ways people actually work usually differs fundamentally from the way organisations describe the work in manuals, training programs or job descriptions. Work always includes the tacit dimension, the practical competency and professional artistry. This underlines the lack of understanding of how learning at the workplace actually takes place. However, there are findings on how work should be shaped to promote learning and quality (Stegmaier, 2000, p.3).

When workers are undertaking their work, they

"do not select a set of appropriate means in relation to an objective and given work, which is separate from their experience. Instead, when workers encounter their work, they frame and set the problem situations of the work through their experience of it" (Sandberg, 2000, p. 52).

This underpins the context-dependent nature of competency and its use through the workers' ways of experiencing that work.

As soon as we separate individuals and work, the individuals' understanding of their work is nullified. Descriptions of competency arising from rationalistic approaches "must" be incomplete and, consequently, misleading as a basis for managing competency in organisations.

These findings complement the Dreyfus & Dreyfus model of skill acquisition and development of competency in suggesting a high level of performance may be attainable through learning at the workplace. The highest level in the Dreyfus model is the expert level. An individual acting as an expert no longer relies on analytic principles (e.g. rules, procedures, definition) to link understanding of a situation to an appropriate action.

Learning at the workplace has important advantages which should not be ignored. However, the development of workplace learning requires organisational leaders to facilitate workplace learning environments and cohesive and interactive work teams who are willing to take risks in their learning and to engage in organisational im-provement. The six dimensions for the shaping of work for a better learning environment can provide valuable orientation in this development.

Different Forms of Learning at the Workplace

The author has undertaken a survey on the "Learning of employees along with accomplishing operational tasks" within enterprises. The survey was supported by the European Community Initiative ADAPT[3] through the European Social Fund. The focus of the survey was wider than "learning during working" or "learning by working". The

---

3   ADAPT = Adaptation of the Workforce to the Industrial Changes. ADAPT followed the main message of the Green Paper „Partnership for a new organization of work". The core is that a better organization of work, based on skill, trust and quality as well as a high level of involvement of workers, can make a valuable contribution to the competitiveness of European firms, to the improvement of the quality of working life and to the employability of the workforce. A new approach to organizing work implies the replacement of hierarchical and rigid structures with others that are more innovative and flexible (Mora et al., 2000, p. 5).

aim was to identify as many facets and trends of "learning at the workplace" as possible (cf. Becker/Spöttl, 2000). The survey concentrated on the daily learning processes critical for the successful accomplishment of a task in a company. This included:

- Learning "on-the-job",

- Learning "on demand",

- Learning by consulting manuals,

- Learning by using databases, the Internet etc.

It is clear that there is no universally valid approach for "learning during work" or "learning at the workplace". Many approaches are possible, each with its own individual and company specific profile.

A survey in micro-companies (less than 10 employees) in Ireland points out that life-long learning (in a sense of learning at the workplace) is normal in these companies. Up to 11 different modes and measures used by employees for learning at the workplace were identified:

- Periodicals,

- Work plans,

- Internet, videos,

- Manuals,

- Problem solving with colleagues,

- Coping with difficult tasks,

- Advice from experts,

- Learning by experience,

- Practise with new equipment,

- Routine tasks are avoided,

- Support of the management (cf. van den Tillaart et al., 1998, p. 47).

These "methods" for learning at the workplace are mainly observed in small enterprises and are applied in very specific situations. A situation-oriented use of selected measures can contribute considerably to the continuing development of employees' competencies.

> "The most important thing is the desire for constant personal improvement. If the worker does not believe in the necessity of training then no kind of formal or informal training has any effect on him. Then, getting in touch with the subject of the work is most important. This comprises seminars of new technology, importer-distributor training of one or more of the mechanics on a certain new model and, finally, training on the actual product itself within the workshop. Team training is the third most important component of learning. All the rest (i.e. manuals, books) only play a supplementary role in the effort to improve and maintain a good level of services in the work" (van den Tillaart et al., 1998, p. 47).

This statement underlines the importance of the shaping of work. It is not learning during the work process that has to be shaped, but the work environment that must be designed to promote learning. The difficulties we are encountering are that the scientific knowledge of the mental processes forming the basis of learning during work is rather limited.

Despite the use of different methods and forms of learning, all are linked to company practice and therefore are accepted by both employees and employers.

The importance of learning at the workplace in small enterprises is also underpinned by a survey carried out in a structurally underdeveloped region in Germany. Workplace learning was the dominant form of learning (43 %), whilst seminars and conferences accounted for only 22 % of learning activities. Learning by adapted further training (14.9 %), career further training (13.7 %) and further training during leisure hours (8.8 %) play only marginal roles (cf. Büchter et al., 2000).

Nevertheless, learning at the workplace is not only important for small enterprises. Large companies consider this form of training as increasingly important. Automobile manufacturers are currently changing their continuing training systems to replace the present theoretically orientated seminar system with continuing training carried out directly at the production level. One of the car manufacturers surveyed completely transformed their continuing training between 1993 and 1998. Within just five years, the 80 % share of seminar training was turned into 80 % of training at the workplace.

Apart from learning at the workplace, other forms of learning were also identified. Product briefings and seminars are still the dominant methods of further training (cf. Table 1). Holistic further training philosophies that consider the qualification level of the employees as important are limited to exceptionally innovative enterprises, usually with a direct link between qualifications and pay (cf. Spöttl et al., 2001). Product related training is often seen as workplace training. This must, however, be questioned given the objectives of "product briefings" which are mainly limited to learning how to deal with specific products.

Development of Expertise via Learning at the Workplace

What is learned at the workplace and what may be learned during the work process also depends on different methods of learning[4]. The overall objective is to promote the following basic competencies:

- Learning to acquire knowledge,
- Learning to act,
- Learning to live with others,
- Life-long learning[5].

The acquisition of non-objectifiable knowledge plays an important role in learning during work processes. In the longer term, experience-based knowledge can have exceptional importance. An example is the acquisition of knowledge which allows a

---

4   Cf. further details by Fischer (2002).
5   This objective is based on the Delors Report of 1996.

worker to repair a fault in a machine based on experience of cause and effect. It could also include interaction with colleagues in order to exchange non-documented data.

Learning during the work process blends practical, acting and theoretical knowledge into expert knowledge. From experience to realization, from knowledge to skills, there is an integration of practical acting in the context of work. And this is what makes an expert. In order to accomplish this objective, a variety of methods have to be deployed and a connection between learning and work has to be practically realized. Space has to be made available for:

- Self-guided learning,
- Autonomous coping with tasks,
- Learning through trial and error,
- Collective exchange of experiences with colleagues,
- Target orientation, planning, execution and control,
- Exploring learning with others.

When these acting spaces and degrees of freedom in terms of time and contents are guaranteed, work integrated learning in the sense described above is possible and facilitates development towards an expert.

The European Approach of the ADAPT Programme – Paving the Way for Learning at the Workplace

As stated previously, learning at the workplace occurs in various operational contexts. 250 out of the 657 German ADAPT projects in the last six years have dealt, more or less intensively, with learning at the workplace. About 40 of these projects concentrated on this topic, whilst 15 could be described as model projects (cf. Becker/Spöttl, 2002). It should be noted that only one of the enterprises involved in the 40 projects employed more than 60 workers. All the other companies had a staff of less than 60, the majority employed 5 to 20 personnel.

Requirements for Learning at the Workplace – An Empirical View

One lesson from looking at the different projects is that successful approaches to learning at the workplace do exist but are often not recognized because they are mistaken or confused for other forms of learning. The following minimum standards may therefore help in identifying workplace learning:

- Learning at the workplace must show a clear delineation from the traditional seminar system.
- There must be a link to learning through work processes.
- Learning concepts coordinated with learning at the workplace must be clearly visible.

Table 1: Further Training Approaches in Enterprises.

Table 1. Further training approaches in enterprises.

	Learning at the workplace	Product-oriented briefings	Product-oriented seminars	Holistic further training philosophies
Objectives	Identify, master and co-shape continuous changes	Master new equipment, new production technologies (be able to operate)	Learning the function, interrelationships of new developments	Further training as a continuing instrument for the improvement of the staff's qualification level linked to a remuneration concept.
Character Focal Points (examples)	Acquisition of production and assembly methods according to assembly optimisation plans, standard working methods. Learning with the aid of multipliers in teams or in groups. Learning on demand (on-the-job).	Situation and product oriented briefings at the workplace, in the company on: new plants/machines/ products, changed processes, current problem solutions, new tasks.	Learning in traditional seminars external to the operational working world. Broad topics: control and digital control technology SPS/BUS systems, hydraulics, pneumatics, electrical technology CNC/CAD FMEA/quality assurance	Finding a correlation between team/group performance and remuneration system via knowledge balances, qualification matrix.
Distribution	In 100 % of the enterprises in certain situations. In 15 % of the enterprises as a further training approach.	100 % of interviewed enterprises.	50 % of enterprises interviewed.	20 % of enterprises interviewed.

There must be a clear connection to organisational and personnel development.

- Theoretical learning in groups and through cooperation must be supported.
- Forms of work organisation have to be identified which explicitly promote learning.
- Applied "new technologies/media" must directly support learning at the workplace.
- There must be innovative models for the involvement and participation of companies and their employees.

Obviously these standards entail a considerable effort in persuading and motivating companies to participate in initiatives for learning at the workplace, to encourage them to further develop already existing "models" and to optimise models for their own operational culture.

It is understandable that especially small enterprises can only engage in experimental and development phases if there is a likelihood of success. This can most often be seen when these companies are convinced that their employees are adequately qualified or that "everything is working just fine". As soon as the qualification deficits become too large and begin to hamper the business process, these companies are no longer prepared to introduce human resource development measures. They try to solve these problems in other ways.

Advantages and Disadvantages of Learning at the Workplace

The arguments for or against learning at the workplace are many and often reflect our own learning experiences. Table 2 compiles the arguments for and against workplace learning based on the experience of the 40 enterprise partners of the ADAPT projects. The companies fear above all that learning might dominate the work process ("companies are not schools") and that productive work may be neglected.

There remains a difference between operational thinking and the idea of a learning organisation. Therefore, it is even more important to pursue learning at the workplace in the sense of an integration of learning and working. There are possibilities to establish an interaction between learning and working which ensure productive work and at the same time do not exclude the further development of staff through learning.

Within this context, the organisation of the work appears as an area of operation that has to be considered in its whole extent. Human capital has become a key factor in competitiveness. The idea that a company is not able to create value in the long term if it does not manage and organise the knowledge and skills of its staff, bearing in mind principles related to salaries, training, loyalty, and working conditions is widespread (cf. Leney et al. 2004).

Table 2: Arguments For and Against Learning at the Workplace.

Arguments against learning at the workplace	Arguments for learning at the workplace
No systematic learning can take place.	Employees stay at the company.
No control of knowledge dissemination is possible.	Learning is undertaken by problem solving.
Every day business prohibits learning.	There is no more "dead knowledge". (problematic work situations may yield successful learning situations).
Acquired knowledge cannot be verified.	
Certification is impossible due to missing instruments.	Acquired knowledge may be immediately applied, is used productively.
Lack of certification prevents promotion to higher salary levels for employees.	Costs are low (no travel expenses, less leave of absence of staff …).
Learning inhibits productive work.	New technologies and working rules are subjects of learning.
There is a lack of didactical teaching aids.	
If learners lack the ability for self-guidance workplace learning can be ineffective.	Learning is integrated into the organisation of the company.
	Learning "on demand" and "just in time" is always possible.
	Learning and operational culture are congruent.
Companies are not schools.	Integration of learning and working.

Learning at the workplace, in the sense of an integration of learning and working, must therefore be comprehensively conceived and must be coordinated with the corporate culture in order to guarantee a high degree of acceptance. The structure of the work organisation, remuneration systems, working conditions etc. must be adapted accordingly.

Employees can adapt to step by step change through learning during work and can contribute to its shaping. When it comes to sudden change, e.g. to the introduction of entirely new technologies and forms of work organization, old competencies become obsolete and are no longer adequate to deal with new work processes. Employees without sufficient general and occupational knowledge cannot meet the new requirements.

Competencies acquired through work cannot easily be documented and are not therefore transparent to potential new employers. Employees who have become qualified through in-company work processes have often had to take lower qualified jobs if they have been forced to seek new employment. This is a long-standing problem which only came to the fore with the structural crisis in major industrial sectors such as the steel industry and which led to wide scale re-employment (cf. Bosch, 2003, 16).

Such situations can be countered with learning at the workplace, provided that work processes are shaped in a way to allow for an acquisition of the necessary know-how and know-that during work at all times. Variety of "learning at the workplace" guarantees the success of human resource development.

The cooperation between the 40 ADAPT projects referred to above and the associated enterprises and their work on the development of approaches for learning at the workplace resulted in five interesting trends[6]. These trends are all marked by very simple structures which may be easily implemented according to corporate cultures and work organisation (cf. Table 3).

These trends underline a great variety of different learning approaches which will become "practice in mixed forms". It must be emphasised that learning at the workplace cannot be systematised through commonly applied learning theories and didactical approaches but requires its own systematisation. This entails a first step towards a way of learning which is oriented towards different corporate cultures and which no longer adheres to the traditional systematic rules. Every company, every form of work organisation and every challenge for personnel development require a specifically adapted response at workplace level.

Nevertheless a characterisation of the trends is possible (cf. Matrix 1). Learning in real situations is closely adapted to corporate cultures, highly context-oriented and thus linked to work processes. This way of learning can seldom – if ever – be formalised.

However, it offers great advantages for the company provided that the supporting instruments are easy to implement. The opposite approach – formalised learning away from the workplace – is generally well structured but does not necessarily provide answers to the needs of the target groups.

Target oriented learning at the workplace is based on an integration of learning and working with a flexible application of different methods and instruments. Therefore, it represents the best compromise between systematised learning and learning in real situations. Partly structured learning at the workplace has the advantage of a link to the work process. It is, however, partly formalised. The most important aim is to maintain a balance between work process orientation and formalisation in order to be able to assess the success of the learning process with regard to the accomplishment of tasks.

Various empirical research underpins this approach (Stegmaier, 2000, p. 193f.). Integrated work and learning environments provide a challenge in the application of learning strategies, in comparison with formal learning in educational institutions. This is especially so as work situations suitable for learning are markedly varied and are thus not transferable. Learning strategies have not only to be carefully planned, they also have to be modified according to the particular situation (cf. Spöttl/ Windelband 2006).

Based on this approach, it is possible to develop a theory to shape learning strategies in a way that they may contribute to human resource development in enterprises.

---

6   Similar trends also could be observed in other European countries such as Sweden, Spain, Great Britain, Greece, Belgium, and France. There are no results available for other countries.

Table 3: Observed Trends in Organisational Learning

Nr.	Trend	Target	Didactics/ methods	Instruments
1	Observation, learning and comprehension	Comprehension and understanding of processes, Acquisition of documentary knowledge and knowledge of rules, standards etc.	Learning with the aid of real work tasks via regulatory theory	Aids for problem solving as hardcopy or multi-media, cartoons and manuals
2	Problem solving at the workplace	Development of situation-oriented competencies for problem solving, Efficient accomplishment of real, problem-based work tasks	Learning on demand in case of problems. Context-oriented support via flexible methods (learning by doing)	Help with problem solving via the Internet, telephone hotlines etc. Cooperation with colleagues
3	Learning during breaks	Acquisition of context-oriented formalised knowledge	Communication-oriented learning by using various instruments.	The Internet as a knowledge platform, data bases (including information and communication technology)
4	Learning in various operational situations and application at own workplace.	Coping with a large variety of tasks in different situations	Application of various learning forms from seminars to breakdown of work processes.	Learning tasks taken from the company, a multitude of problem-oriented materials.
5	Individualised, situation-related learning.	Solving of complex situation-specific tasks "Learn only what is needed"	Individualised learning with various learning forms/ mix of learning forms.	Operational situations, colleagues, study corners, learning office, etc. …

Summary

Individual projects on learning at the workplace and individual trends differ. Each project, each approach corresponds in a particular way to operational challenges. It is this synergy that provides the opportunities for different approaches and different projects to succeed in developing learning at the workplace.

Matrix 1: Characterisation of Learning at the Workplace

	strongly developed	Target-oriented learning at the workplace Integrated learning at the workplace	Learning in real situations Learning from problems of the work process
Learning culture in enterprises	none	Formalised learning Learning in seminars and at the workplace	Partly structured learning at the workplace Learning through work tasks or work orders
		in the surroundings	**directly**
		Learning in the work process	

It is possible to shape workplace learning in a way that both learners and companies can see as promoting successful development. "Adapted concepts" can bring people, company organisation and learning together. In order to achieve this objective, and to develop guidelines, theoretical approaches are needed; however, this does not imply formal systematisation. Company-oriented learning cultures must be developed which allow for different learning concepts to be shaped for application in different workplaces. This also includes the development of instruments and materials.

A crucial pre-requisite is, however, that learning at the workplace must be welcomed and supported by companies instead of being thwarted. This means that the pressure for results must not be too high and inhibit the development of free spaces for integrated work and learning.

References

Becker, M. & Spöttl, G. (2002). *Concepts for the Practice.* NU-ADAPT, Bonn.

Bosch, G. (2003). *Betriebliche Reorganisation und neue Lernkulturen.* In: Bsirske, Frank / Endl, Hans-L. / Schröder, Lothar / Schwemmle, Michael (Hrsg.): *Wissen ist was wert: Wissensmanagement.* Hamburg: VSA-Verl., S. 118-129.

Büchter, K.; Christe, G.; & Jankofsky, B. (2000). *Klein- und Mittelbetriebe im Strukturwandel.* IWAQ-Studie, Oldenburg.

Butt, Wai Ch. (2005). *K-Workers, Key to our Survival.* New Straits Times. October 8.

Dreyfus, H.L. & Dreyfus, S.E. (2000). *Mind over Machine. The Power of Human Intuition and Experience in the Era of the Computer.* Free Press, New York.

Fischer, M. (2002). *Die Entwicklung von Arbeitsprozesswissen durch Lernen im Arbeitsprozess – Theoretische Annahmen und empirische Befunde.* In Fischer, M. & Rauner, F. (Hrsg.): Lernfeld: Arbeitsprozess. NOMOS, Baden-Baden.

Gerber, R. & Lankshear, C.(Ed.). (2000). *Training for a Smart Workforce.* Routledge; London, New York.

Gerstenmaier, J. (1999). Die *Bedeutung bereichsspezifischen Wissens für Wissenserwerb und Leistung.* GdWZ 10, Heft 2, 1999, S. 65-67.

Leney, T.; Coles, M.; Grollmann, Ph.; Vilu, R. (2004): *Handreichungen zur Szenarioentwicklung.* CEDFOP Dossier series 7, Luxembourg.

Livingstone, D.W. (1999). *Informelles Lernen in der Wissensgesellschaft.* QEUM-report, Heft 60, p. 65-90.

Mora, F. et al. (2000). *New Forms of Work Organisation and the Information Society.* ADAPT & EMPLOYMENT Community Initiatives, European Communities, Luxembourg.

Sandberg, I. (2000). *Competency – the Basis for a Smart Workforce.* In: Gerber, R. & Lankshear, C. (Ed.). Traning for a Smart Workforce. Routledge: London, New York, p. 47-72.

Spöttl, G. (2002). *Training and Education in and for Small and Medium Size Enterprises.* biat: Flensburg, Kuala Lumpur.

Spöttl, G.; Holm, C.; & Windelband, L. (2001). *Ermittlung von Qualifikationsanforderungen für Dienstleistungen des produzierenden Gewerbes am Beispiel der Metallbranche.* BIBB-Studie, Flensburg.

Spöttl, G. (2004). Promoting Learning at the Workplace: *Challenges in Shaping the Work Environment.* In: Fischer, M.; Boreham, N.; Nyhan, B. (Ed.). European Perspectives on Learning at Work: the Acquisition of Work Process Knowledge. CEDEFOP Ref. Series 56, Luxembourg, p.186-195.

Spöttl, G.; Windelband, L. (2006): *Employment research method for early recognition of skills needs.* European Journal of Vocational Training. No. 39, 2006/3, p. 62-79.

Staudt, W. & Kriegesmann, B. (1999). *Weiterbildung: Ein Mythos zerbricht. Der Widerspruch zwischen überzogenen Erwartungen und Misserfolgen der Weiterbildung.* In: Staudt, E. (Hrsg.). Berichte aus der angewandten Innovationsforschung. Nr. 178, Bochum.

Stegmair, R. (2000). *Kompetenzentwicklung durch arbeitsintegriertes Lernen in der Berufsbildung.* Universität Heidelberg, Dissertation.

Tillaart, van den, H.; Berg, van den, S.; & Warmerdam, J. (1998). *Work and Learning in Micro-Repair Enterprises.* Cedefop, Thessaloniki.

Education and Training in Private-Public-Partnership: The German Experience

Hermann W. Schmidt

Education and Training – The Investment

A country without natural resources, Germany's only choice, in order to compete successfully in a global market, is to invest in its own people. In the early seventies the country decided to educate and train all school leavers who were not college or university bound.

There Have to Be Options

The broad consensus in society was that this ambitious aim could not be reached by just prolonging obligatory schooling up to twelve or thirteen years. A broad campaign "to send children to better schools for longer" and "to improve the dual training system to world class standards" was successful. In-company training was made part of the education system, and employers and trade unions, representing the world of work as "social partners", were invited by the government to take partial responsibility for educational planning and standard setting. A Federal Institute for Vocational Training (Bundesinstitut fuer Berufsbildung – BIBB) was founded to do research and development; providing a common platform for employers, trade unions and government to develop common scenarios of future education and training in Germany.

Parity of Esteem

Since 1970, the proportion of school leavers entering the Dual System of education and training, with companies providing instruction and colleges of further education providing day release, rose from 50 % to almost 70 % in 2000. At the same time the number of students in full time colleges of further education doubled and the number of students holding a baccalaureate or A-level certificate tripled. Today a great number of students in secondary education earn at least two qualifications; one at full time school and another one in the Dual System. One third of students at college or university have gone through a two to three year training period prior to their studies. The Dual System has gained in reputation and recognition, not only in corporate Germany, but in society as a whole as an alternative career pathway.

Transition from School to Work

As a result of the educational campaign, the average age of a trainee entering the Dual System rose from fifteen and half to eighteen years old within three decades. This is due to the fact that a large proportion of students had to improve their school records to get the traineeship they wanted because of rising requirements in vocational education. Although the Dual System does not require formal entrant's qualifications, companies who offer training places often do.

In the year 2000, 97 % of each age cohort leaving obligatory school entered a track of higher or further education and 85 % achieved one or more qualifications. Since the number of untrained personnel in employment is forecast to drop below 10 % by 2010 there is still a wide gap to be filled.

Challenges and Responses

The technical, economic, organisational and political changes that have shaken all economies of the world during the past decade gave rise to a broad national debate in Germany regarding whether or not the Dual System of education and training would be "future proof". Was it not too highly regulated? Would its occupational focus respond adequately to the challenges of process oriented work organisation? Should we not modularise our occupational pathways and introduce national vocational qualifications, recognising that the concept of "training occupations" is outdated?

The "Alliance for Work, Vocational Training and Competitiveness", which is chaired by the Federal Chancellor and comprises social partner and government representatives, responded in 1999. The concept of a broad basic training occupation remains at the core of the Dual System but measures have been undertaken to make the system more flexible:

- The procedure to develop and update training standards has been de-regulated and shortened.

- A reform of assessment in the Dual System has been launched: assessment has become more process oriented; the learner's individual portfolio will state the outcomes of learning stages and will not leave those who failed without any certificate; strong efforts are made to "Europeanise" individual portfolios despite the different education systems.

- New "training occupations" (some 40 since 1995) to serve the needs of the new as well as the old economy have been developed, i.e. in the field of information & communication, media and service – some of them in a record time of eight months.

- A system of "early identification of change in job requirements" has been installed where researchers and practitioners jointly try to distinguish changes that are likely to be long lasting and will have an impact on education and training from those which will soon be outdated and do not deserve to become part of a standard.

- The core of an occupational standard, which is looked upon as a longer term basis for education and training, is separated from "additional competencies" which are sector or company specific and are subject to frequent changes.

- Standards, contents and assessment of initial training in the Dual System and in further education and training are no longer separately discussed, although the flexibility of further training was maintained.

The ability of the Dual System's stakeholders, private and public, to keep up with change and to renew and modernise the system has been proven. This ensures that the system meets the requirements of the labour market, as well as the expectations of a young person with respect to the development of her/his own personality and career, giving us hope to master the challenges of the future.

Who Benefits from Education and Training in Private-Public-Partnership?

1. The Learner

Education systems must, first of all, serve the needs of the learner. It is the purpose of any Education & Training (E&T) system to prepare young people to find their vocational or professional role and position and to act in this role independently. It must enable them to develop their personality with all its talents and abilities so as to play their role as citizens in a democratic society and as a team member in the work force.

Of course, E&T systems in private-public partnerships have to pursue the same purpose. It is a well known phenomenon that a great number of students get tired of school when they are in their mid-teens. They prefer learning environments that provide opportunities for action rather than listening and writing in the classroom. E&T systems which include learning at the workplace or in other real life situations improve the motivation of young learners because they offer opportunities for action. The learning programme transfers responsibility onto the learner and requires information, planning, decision making, and occupational and self-control skills which are an integral part of the learning process and are not directed by the teacher. This learning arrangement combines learning and earning (trainee remuneration scale) at an age where financial independence from parents is highly appreciated.

2. The Training Enterprise

Employers will not get involved in an E&T private-public partnership for social purposes or welfare reasons (see Figure 1). Those who expect this misunderstand the role of employers in private-public partnerships. Unless employers act in a strictly economical way when they decide to train young people for their future workforce their efforts will not last long. If the employer does not consider the investment into training to have at least the same value as other capital investment it will be rated as a waste of money. Employers must expect a return on investment, whether it is in capital assets or in human resources.

The main reasons for employers to invest in E&T are:

- To gain a steady inflow of a young employable workforce (2-5 % per year for larger companies) with a corporate identity;

- Saving costs: advertising and hiring costs, induction costs for newly hired workers and costs for badly chosen employees who do not fit in the company or team;

- The win-win experience of a "learning and training company" which gains a reputation in the community for training employees' children and which copes successfully with the problems of further training, constantly updating its strategies for life long learning of older members of the workforce.

Figure 1: Characteristics of the Dual VET-System in Germany

Characteristics of the Dual VET-System in Germany

TRAINEES / STUDENTS:

- are trained in a company (workplace / workshop) for 3 to 4 days per week; attend a further education college for 1 to 2 days per week,
- some 1.7 million in two to three year courses, on average two thirds of an age cohort, some 60% are men and 40% women,
- receive remuneration which is approximately 1/3 of a skilled worker's salary.

"TRAINING COMPANIES":

- some 500,000 provide VET, approximately 1 million meet the requirements of a company accredited for training, the total number of companies is approximately 2.5 million,
- large companies train approximately 20% of all trainees; the majority is trained in small and medium enterprises,
- make work arrangements for 2 to 3 years of systematic training and pay remuneration.

---

3. The Society as a Whole

Confronted with the global problems of an unfavourable outlook for unskilled labour, rising unemployment and crime rates, there is nothing more worthwhile for society than to invest in E&T. But even if a country decides to train ALL non-college bound school-leavers, it is unlikely to do this just by prolonging school beyond the age of eighteen. Taxpayers cannot be expected to bear the cost of buildings, equipment and the teaching force, nor can the willingness of all young people to remain at school beyond twelve years be expected.

Societies that set up an E&T system in private-public partnership gain:

- The opportunity to educate and train ALL school-leavers,

- A model of sharing costs with the private sector that cuts the taxpayers' education cost burden down to one third of the total E&T cost, depending on the rate of enterprise involvement,

- Employers as partners in educational planning and for setting and updating high level E&T standards,

- Stability in education and training policy because of strong stakeholder involvement.

What Were the Pre-Conditions for the Dual Education and Training System in Germany?

Germany is a country without major natural resources. In the early twentieth century industry adopted the country's traditional E&T system, which was rooted in the medieval crafts and guilds E&T system. But it was not until the 1960s that Germany decided to educate and train all school leavers. The Basic Training Act was passed in the Bundestag (the Federal Parliament) in 1969. It was based on the following assumptions:

- A broad consensus in society to educate and train ALL school leavers and a strong will to allocate more money to education and training,

- The presence of strong "social partners", employers and trade unions, who are the backbones of the company-training-system,

- A top down strategic decision that brought together the federal government, the education ministers of the federal states (*Land*), employers and trade unions to implement an improved Dual System of E&T with high standards and excellent delivery,

- The readiness of the government to accept the private sector as a partner in education on an equal footing,

- The readiness of the private sector to accept national E&T standards set by government and external quality control of their activities in initial training,

- The chambers of commerce and industry to be endowed with the rights of a public authority for E&T and to act on behalf of the government by accrediting training companies, monitoring and assessing training outcomes, and issuing certificates,

- E&T research and development to be indispensable tools for the improvement and further development of E&T in Germany and to facilitate stakeholder cooperation.

The Main Rules of the Basic Training Act of 1969[1]

The history of the Basic Training Act dates back to the early days of the first democratic German parliament in 1919 when the draft of an In-Company Training Act was introduced. Diverging interests of trade unions, employers and related political parties prevented the act from being passed. Fifty years later the first grand coalition of the country's largest political parties in post-war Germany, the Social Democratic Party (SPD) and the Christian Democratic Party (CDU), managed to reach a consensus in the shape of the Basic Training Act of 1969 despite many heated arguments. This broad political consensus has given stability and sustainability to the system throughout the past decades.

The main new features that were introduced by this Training Act established a private-public partnership in E&T planning with employers and trade unions. This grew to become a de-facto co-determination on E&T standards, curricula and assessment, and a new type of E&T research and development in private-public partnership.

---

1   A new/ revised Training Act was approved by the German Parliament in 2005.

The Basic Training Act set the stage for:

- Clear funding arrangements: private enterprises are responsible for in-company-training and remuneration, they guarantee day-release, they pay a levy to the chamber, the government takes responsibility for schooling (state governments), E&T research, programmes for the handicapped and E&T innovation (federal government),

- An organisational infrastructure: provided by the chambers of industry and commerce, crafts, medical doctors, lawyers and others, each of them acting as a public authority for training,

- E&T system components (standard criteria, legal training contract criteria, prior learning accreditation, duration of training, day release schooling, assessment and certification, remuneration of trainees etc.),

- A Federal Institute for Vocational Training (BIBB) which will be described in detail later.

The "Key Players" in the Dual E&T System in Germany

1. Training Companies

Some 500,000 companies and public authorities in all sectors of the economy provide some 1.7 million training places. This half a million companies represent roughly 50 % of all companies that meet the requirements of a "training company" (1 million out of some 2.5 million companies that represent corporate Germany). They provide structured systematic training for two to three years.

A total of approximately 20 % of all 1.7 million trainees are trained in the larger companies. The great majority are trained in small and medium sized enterprises (SMEs).

Training companies provide work arrangements for two or three years of systematic training according to national standards, conclude legal training contracts, provide licensed trainers, enrol the trainee at the chamber, pay remuneration, bear training costs and give day release for the trainee to attend VET institutes.

2. Trainee/ Student/ Apprentice

There are some 1.6 million trainees in two to three years' training courses, on average approximately two thirds of an age cohort[2]. Of these about 60 % are men and 40 % are women. Apprentices are trained in the company for three to four days a week and attend a VET institution on one or two days per week (or in a blocked form – 13 weeks per year)(Statistisches Bundesamt 2007).

Trainees receive a remuneration which is approximately one third of a skilled employee's salary within that particular sector (farming, metal industry etc). The average age of trainees is 18 years, which shows that quite a number improve their school results by attending further education prior to their traineeship.

---

2   In 2006, exactly 59 per cent of the relevant age cohort moved into the Dual System.

3. VET institutions

There are roughly 1700 VET institutions in the country. They are maintained by cities or communities and are usually equipped with workshops, laboratories or offices where real work situations can be simulated or demonstrated. Some 90,000 teachers holding relevant university degrees are teaching dual system trainees as well as full time students. Teachers are employed and paid by the state (*Land*) in which their college is located.

4. Chambers of Commerce and Industry

There are some 430 chambers in all sectors of the economy, predominantly in industry, commerce and crafts, but also for medical doctors and lawyers (through the training of assistants). Membership with a chamber is mandatory for all companies.

Chambers act as a public authority in all training matters: they accredit "training companies", advise them on training matters, cooperate with VET institutions in their district, they are able to use training bodies comprising employers, trade unions and teachers, which advise chambers and assess trainees and trainers. The chambers record training contracts, organise assessments and issue certificates for trainees and trainers.

5. The Social Partners: Employers and Trade Unions

The social partners are the pillars on which the Dual System is based. Employers and trade unions act on all levels (federal, state, and local) as driving agents within the Dual System: they advise governments and public authorities, they decide on E&T research programmes of the Federal Institute for Vocational Training (BIBB), they prepare E&T standards for all training occupations, and they maintain agencies to act on their behalf in E&T planning and policy making.

Training Cost

Highly industrialised economies are drastically reducing their unskilled labour in their transformation to knowledge societies. Investment in human resources has become even more important than capital investment. Whether or not to invest in the workforce is not the question. However, it is a strategic decision whether to invest into initial AND continuing training or allocate all training investment to the adult workforce. Corporate Germany has decided to take the first alternative and keeps on doing so (cf. Berufsbildungsbericht 2006).

We have seen that companies that train young workers not only *spend* money, they also *save* costs arising from the hiring, firing and induction of newly hired employees who do not know the company. Training costs in the Dual System of Germany vary signify-cantly from larger companies with training workshops and full time instructors, to SMEs where the workplace is the only training area and the team members are the only trainers. They vary from sector to sector (e.g. hair dresser, mechanic) and even regio-nally. Nevertheless, it is feasible to break-even in the course of training, even for larger companies, by taking into account the productivity of the trainee. Usually, larger companies have a long term perspective in training their young workforce and therefore expect a return on investment later than SMEs.

A rough breakdown of training costs shows that personnel costs are predominant:

- 50 per cent training personnel,
- 40 per cent trainee remuneration,
- 10 per cent training equipment, material, books, travelling cost etc.

Drawbacks

The Dual System in private-public partnership suffered, like all other E&T systems, its drawbacks. Major deficiencies arise from communication problems between the world of work and the world of education. They remain different worlds, even if linked together in private-public partnership. Employers, though experienced over the past decades in describing the needs and outcomes they expect from E&T, have problems when trying to define exactly what is outdated and what "new standards" in terms of skills, knowledge, abilities and competencies should now be adopted.

Employers, trade unions, government and colleges have been blamed by the public for the late reaction of the Dual System to the technological and organisational challenges of the evolving knowledge society.

In many cases, communications between company instructors and college teachers still neglect to focus on the learner.

Over the past years even a record high offer of 630,000 training places (in 2000) fell short of the demand of 650,000 and more. In 2006, 576,378 new contracts were signed (cf. BIBB 2006).

Even sixteen years after the reunification of Germany, the country has failed to build a Dual System of training in East Germany that is equivalent to the one in the West. Only high government (federal and state) subsidies to companies and grants for additional full time training in group training centres has made it possible to meet the demand. The East German economy still lacks the small and medium sized enterprise structure that ensures a great number of training places in the West. Hence, eastern Germany suffers a brain drain of young people moving west because of the lack of training places at home.

The Federal Institute for Vocational Training

(Bundesinstitut für Berufsbildung – BIBB)

1. The Idea Behind the Organisation

The main purpose of the Basic Training Act of 1969 was the overall reform of the traditional German training system; governed by the principles of participation and consensus in private-public partnership, research based innovation and improvement.

Thus, in the late sixties, two research institutes were established which focused on the workforce:

- The Institute for Labour Market and Occupational Research (Institut für Arbeitsmarkt- und Berufsforschung, IAB) – incorporated as part of the German Employment Office at Nuremberg,

- The Institute for Vocational Training (Bundesinstitut für Berufsbildung, BIBB) in Berlin.

Because of the partnership between social partners and the federal government in the labour market as well as in vocational training policy the newly founded institutes comprised the stakeholders as board members and partners in research. In this respect they are quite different from any other research institution.

The main political function of these tri-partite boards is the frequent discussion of the development of E&T and the labour market in Germany. They decide on future scenarios in this field, basing these decisions on current research. They provide support for these developments in companies and the labour market.

The Federal Institute for Vocational Training (BIBB), which has moved to Bonn, is both a public authority in private-public partnership, a research institute, an E&T programme agency and a knowledge broker, and a platform for stakeholders of the Dual System of training.

2. The BIBB: A Platform for Stakeholders

Today the Institute is governed by a management board comprised of four interest groups: the employers, the trade unions, the federal government, and the state governments.

Employers, trade unions and state officials advise federal government (the Ministries of Research and Education, of Economy, of Labour, of the Interior, and of Family and Youth) on all E&T policy matters. Among other matters they approve the annual "Report on the state of E&T in Germany" which is prepared by the Institute and presented to parliament by the Minister of Research and Education in April each year. The board as a whole decides on the Institute's research programme and its corresponding budget.

The President of the BIBB, who directs some 400 staff (including around 150 scientific personnel), is a civil servant who acts autonomously in his professional duties and cannot be dismissed by government. The legal supervision and political responsibility for the budget lies with the Ministry of Research and Education. The funding of the

BIBB reflects the federal government's firm intention to let social partners take responsibility in the Institute. The BIBB is 100 % federally funded although the federal government only holds one quarter of the votes on the Board.

3. The BIBB: A Research Institute

In line with the overall concept of a private-public partnership, the Board decides on all research projects and studies carried out by the BIBB. There are, of course, contradicting views within the board regarding the role of the federal government in funding BIBB. There are different interest areas where both common and divergent interests occur. For example, there are cases where the majority of stakeholders do not want to have research done, despite the federal government and the BIBB itself have good reasons for clarification through research.

The pros and cons of diverging interests when dealing with this type of research cannot be denied. But those who argue that the "spiritus rector" of traditional research at universities is entirely devoted to finding the truth, to unravelling the secrets of nature and society, and that there is no room for the influence of interest groups, do not tell the whole truth about university research.

Research at the BIBB has to serve the needs of the learning workforce and the stakeholders. It has a responsibility to adapt the system to technological and organisational change and improve the quality of training. Long term and strategic studies are necessary, as well as short term advice, to make planning processes reliable and their results sustainable.

Often the workplace is the field of research and practitioner involvement is more than welcome. Researchers who get involved in these types of studies must not only be professionals in the methodology of research but must also be knowledgeable about the world of work and able to communicate with practitioners about their problems. This type of researcher is hard to find.

Research findings are the raw material for political advice, reports, quality assurance, updating standards and curricula, innovation of assessment, international benchmarking, government and European Union (EU) programmes, new strategies in HRD and many other purposes.

4. The BIBB: A Programme Agency & Knowledge Broker

Being in permanent contact with the leading training companies and colleges of further education of the country, the BIBB collects, analyses and publishes data, research findings, and good/best practice examples and discusses them with the national and international E&T community at conferences and workshops. As a knowledge broker in E&T, the BIBB has become a recognised Centre of Expertise and is an ideal agency for both national and EU-programmes.

The BIBB's main programme is the development and updating of national occupational standards (occupational characteristics, objectives and content of training, requirements for assessment etc.). This is conducted in collaboration with social partners and state educators who design college curricula according to the federal standards.

Inter-firm or group training centres support small enterprises with their initial and further training programmes. Some 600 of these centres have been established throughout the country during the last thirty years with strong federal funding (50 to 80%). The centres are usually maintained by the chambers as their support with systematic training courses is crucial to the success of small companies' training efforts. The BIBB, on behalf of the federal government, has supported the planning and funding of these centres since 1977.

An E&T innovation programme awards and funds innovative E&T schemes in companies (federal government, since 1972). The programme is planned, carried out and monitored by the BIBB which also publishes the results on behalf of the Ministry of Education. Pilot projects usually run over a period of four years.

Since the mid-eighties the BIBB, on behalf of the ministry, has run EU programmes that serve to spread cross-border innovations in E&T between companies and educational institutions and that support the exchange of trainees between countries. Since EU countries have agreed not to harmonise their education systems, these programmes pursue the purpose of creating a European innovation, communication and collaboration culture in E&T.

References

Bundesinstitut für Berufsbildung (2006). *BIBB-Erhebung zum 30.09.2006*. Bonn.

Bundesministerium für Bildung und Forschung (2006): *Berufsbildungsbericht 2006*. Bonn, Berlin.

Statistisches Bundesamt (2007): *Bildung und Kultur. Berufliche Bildung*. Wiesbaden.

The Employer's Role in Developing Skills for the New Economy in Australia

Andy Smith

Since 1989 the Australian Bureau of Statistics (ABS) has conducted five surveys of employer training expenditure (ABS, 1990a, 1991, 1994a, 1997, 2003). The original survey conducted as a pilot in 1989 indicated that only 22 per cent of Australian employers carried out any form of training for their employees and that an average of 2.2 per cent of payroll costs was invested in training activities with employees receiving, on average, 22 hours of training per annum. This data together with the results from some international comparisons of incentive schemes to promote higher levels of enterprise investment in training provided a significant part of the case for the then federal Labor government enacting the Training Guarantee Scheme in 1990. This scheme operated from 1990 to 1996 (although it was technically suspended in 1994) and required Australian enterprises with payroll costs of over A$200,000[1] to spend at least 1.5 per cent of their payroll on the provision of "structured" training for their employees or pay an equivalent levy to the Australian Taxation Office. Assessments of the effectiveness of the Training Guarantee in raising the level of training expenditure in Australia vary but it is generally accepted that the scheme failed to lift training provision for the majority of employees in any significant or lasting fashion (Teicher, 1995). Subsequent iterations of the Employer Training Expenditure survey (TES) have tended to confirm the original rather gloomy assessment of the state of enterprise training in Australia. Table 1 summarises the data from the first four TES surveys and shows that although training expenditure appeared to increase to 1993, it had retreated by 1996.

Table 1: Employer Training Expenditure

	1989	1990	1993	1996
% Employers reporting training expenditure	22	24	25	18
% Payroll Spent				
Private Sector	1.7	2.2	2.6	2.3
Public Sector	3.3	3.2	3.4	3.2
Total	*2.2*	*2.6*	*2.9*	*2.5*
Average expenditure per employee (A$)	133	163	191	186
Average training hours per employee	5.5	5.9	5.6	4.9

Source: Australian Bureau of Statistics 1990a, 1991, 1994a, 1997a

---

[1] appr. € 120,000 (2007)

Employer size correlates closely with the incidence of training in enterprises. In 1996, 88.3 per cent of large enterprises (100 or more employees) provided structured training compared to only 13.4 per cent of small enterprises (less than 20 employees). The 2002 data indicates an increase in the incidence of training in all size categories with 98 per cent of large organisations, 70 per cent of medium sized and 39 per cent of small organisations reporting the provision of structured training (ABS, 2003). Spending on training also varies considerably by sector and industry. In 1996, public sector organisations spent 3.2 per cent of payroll compared with their private sector counter-parts who spent 2.3 per cent. However, the increase from 1989 to 1996 was almost entirely accounted for by the private sector which improved its performance by over 30 per cent, whilst public sector spending as a percentage of payroll remained fairly static. Variation across industry sectors is also apparent, with air transport, mining and communications spending well over the average whilst manufacturing, retail and recreation and personal services spent considerably less than the average. The data from the Training Expenditure surveys prompted commentators to draw the conclusion that Australian employer commitment to training has declined since the abolition of the Training Guarantee in the mid-1990s. For instance, Cully and Richardson (2002) sum-marise their evidence on employer contributions to continuing training thus:

> "Of most concern must be the evidence we have provided that suggests employer contributions to continual vocational training have fallen since the abandonment of the Training Guarantee. To reiterate, there was an 11 per cent fall in employer training expenditure (as a percentage of payroll costs) between 1993 and 1996 and a 4 per cent fall in hours of continuing training provided by employers between 1997 and 2001" (p.37).

They conclude

> "In retrospect, however, what we have witnessed over the 1990s is many employers pursuing short-term self-interest. Smaller employers reduced their investment in training, hoping to free ride on the efforts of others" (p. 46).

A more trenchant critique of employer investment in training, based on the training expenditure figures, has been mounted by Richard Hall and his colleagues at ACIRRT (Hall et al, 2002). In a paper for the Düsseldorf Skills Foundation, Hall et al argue cogently that there has been a flight of employers from training since the repeal of the Training Guarantee Act in 1996. This, combined with Australia's poor comparative per-formance on investment in knowledge, education and the creation of high skill jobs, they argue., means that the Australian economy is in a low skills equilibrium (Finegold and Soskice, 1988) and there is little evidence of strong training culture amongst Australian employers.

However, these are very broad claims to be basing on a selective interpretation of the employer training statistics. It is far from clear that this pessimistic view of the state of industry training in Australia is justified given the range of data now available on the incidence of enterprise training. The ABS conduct two other surveys which present data on industry training – the Employer Training Practices Survey (ABS, 1994b, 1998) and the Survey of Education and Training Experience (ABS, 1990b, 1994c, 1998, 2002). The Survey of Education and Training Experience (SET) and its forerunners is a household survey sampling some 20,000 dwellings and collecting data on all individuals aged from 15 to 64 years for the previous year. The results from the 1997 SET show that in 1997, 80.2 per cent of workers received some form of training. On-the-job training was the most common form of training with 71.6 per cent of workers receiving this type of training. The incidence of in-house training in organisations was far less with only 33 per cent of workers receiving this form of training. About 16 per cent of workers were studying for an educational qualification. However, like the figures on training expenditure, there is considerable variation between industries on the type of training received by employees. Employees in the utilities, communications or service industries were more likely to receive training than those in transport, manufacturing or agriculture. The results of the three surveys for employee training to 1997 are summarised in Table 2.

Table 2: Individuals' Experience of Training 1989-1997

Activity	1989	1993	1997
Some training undertaken	79.0	85.8	80.2
Studied in previous calendar year	16.8	18.6	15.8
In-house training course	34.9	31.3	33.0
External training course	9.8	11.8	20.0
On-the-job training	71.8	81.8	71.6

Source: Australian Bureau of Statistics 1998

The data from SET display some interesting contrasts with the TES data. The most obvious difference is that the experience of training for individual workers is far higher than the TES data might lead one to expect. Over the 1990s, 80 per cent or more of workers have undertaken some training. Although the most common experience is of on-the-job training, over 30 per cent of workers have received in-house training – very similar to the "structured" training definition used in the TES. Also, the pattern of provision has changed during the period 1989-1997 in different ways to the pattern of training expenditure from the TES. Whereas the overall incidence of training and of on-the-job training rose in the early 1990s and fell away later in the decade, in-house or structured training increased since 1993 and participation in external training courses almost doubled during the period.

Data from 2001 (ABS, 2002), shows that the incidence of employer sponsored training appears to be still increasing. The proportion of Australian workers undertaking work related training grew from 30 per cent of the workforce in 1993 to 45 per cent in 2001. 37 per cent of workers completed at least one work related training course in 2001 and the proportion of workers completing on-the-job training grew from 65 per cent in 1996 to 69 per cent in 2000. Despite the apparent decline in employer training expenditure since the mid 1990s, the majority of Australian workers claim they are receiving some form of training from their employers and many are undertaking formal, off-the-job training in their firms.

These figures complement the data for overall enrolments in the Australian vocational and education training system which show that the numbers undertaking a VET course have increased by almost 60 per cent in the last 10 years to over 1.75 million in 2001 to the point where over 12 per cent of the Australian population undertake a VET course each year (NCVER, 2002). Moreover, this participation involves students from all age groups, not just those who are engaged in entry-level training. So, it is those within the workplace as much as those negotiating entry to the workplace who are participating in vocational education increasing numbers.

The increasing incidence of in-house training contrasts sharply with the TES data that shows a decline in expenditure on structured training over the same period. Despite the differences in definitions between in-house training in the SET and structured training in the TES, the SET data suggest that the provision of off-the-job training courses on the employers' premises has increased since 1993.

More evidence of the widespread provision of industry training can be gained from the Employer Training Practices Survey (TPS). The TPS is a qualitative survey that gathers information on the type and extent of training provided by enterprises to their employees. Data is collected for a full year rather than for three months as is the case for the TES. Two Training Practices surveys have been carried out (ABS, 1994b, 1997) covering the years 1993 and 1996. In 2002, the Training Practices Survey was carried out in combination with the Training Expenditure Survey in a new survey – the Training Expenditure and Practices Survey (ABS 2003). The Training Practices Survey was administered to the same population as the TES so the data is comparable between the two surveys. However, the data from the 2002 survey is not fully comparable with the previous years. The results from the 1997 TPS show that 61 per cent of all employers provided training to their employees during 1996. This increased to 81 per cent in the 2002 survey. 35 per cent provided structured training whilst 53 per cent provided unstructured training in 1996, increasing to 41 per cent and 79 per cent respectively in 2002. As with training expenditure, the incidence of enterprise training in the TPS varies considerably with size. In 1996, 99 per cent of large enterprises provided training whilst 57 per cent of small employers provided training for their employees. The provision of structured training follows the same pattern with 93 per cent of large enterprises providing structured training and 30 per cent of small enterprises. By 2002, this had increased to 98 per cent of large enterprises and 39 per cent of small enterprises. The TPS data also shows that the low incidence of training provision amongst small enterprises is concentrated in the micro-business end of the spectrum – those enterprises employing fewer than five people, including those businesses that have no employees and represent about half of all small businesses. The figures for small business from the 1996 survey are summarised in Table 3. However, it needs to be acknowledged that small business operators have consistently claimed that the orthodox provision of vocational education through taught courses fails to meet their needs (Coopers and Lybrand, 1994). Among their concerns is that small businesses are not smaller versions of large enterprises (Kempnich *et al*, 1999). Much of the vocational education provision in Australia seems to be directed towards large enterprises and their needs.

Table 3: Percentage of Small Business Enterprises Providing Training

Type of training	1-4 employees	5-9 employees	10-19 employees	All small business
Structured training	20	43	60	30
Unstructured training	38	65	78	49
All training	45	74	86	57

Source: ABS 1998

Despite the similarity in the pattern of training provision, however, there is a remarkable difference in the incidence of training provided by the TES and the TPS. In almost every case, the incidence of structured training detected by the TPS appears to be about double that detected by the TES. 35 per cent of enterprises report providing structured training to their employees in the TPS compared to only 17.7 per cent of enterprises in the TES. 30 per cent of all small enterprises provided structured training in the TPS compared to 13.4 per cent in the TES. For larger enterprises, the figures are more comparable. Nevertheless, 99 per cent of enterprises provided structured training in the TPS compared with 88.3 per cent in the TES.

There are some differences between the two surveys that might account for some of these divergent findings. In particular, the TES provides data for only one quarter in the year whereas the TPS gathers data on training activity for the preceding 12 months. The TPS collects a broader range of data than the TES with the emphasis on qualitative data rather than the strictly defined quantitative data of the TES. Thus, the TPS may allow the collection of data on training activities that cannot be fitted into the strict definitional guidelines of the TES. Further evidence of the more all-embracing approach of the TPS is provided by the slightly different definitions of structured training used in the two surveys. In both surveys the definition of structured training allows the inclusion of on-the-job training. However, in the TES on-the-job training is restricted to training "associated with the assessment of accredited competency-based skills". This definition severely limits the amount of on-the-job training captured under the definition of structured training in the TES and may help to account for the lower incidence of structured training reported. Thus, the TPS appears to be a better guide to the true level of structured training provided within enterprises. What seems significant is that employees report higher levels of in-house training than do their employers. This may well be a product of the employers responding to surveys that constrain the reporting of training activity, because their definitions are more narrowly defined. However, it might be expected that employers would seek to amplify their efforts. Conversely, those in the workplace do not always acknowledge on the job training when a peer or supervisor provides it. So, there are at the least two realities: the employers and employees. Employees may be providing a more comprehensive picture based upon their learning experiences. This presents itself as a useful way of transcending training provided through structured and credentialed courses, and those other kinds of learning experiences that individuals encounter in workplaces. Ultimately, perhaps, this is the most important measure.

Further support for a more optimistic view of the incidence of industry training in Australia is provided by the Business Longitudinal Survey (BLS) (ABS, 1999). This survey comprises a composite of data gathered from a sample of business on the ABS business register. The BLS gathers data primary on business and financial performance of enterprises but also includes some simple questions on the provision of training to employees. In 1997/98, the BLS data indicated that 54 per cent of enterprises provided training to their employees and 23 per cent provided structured training. Whilst these figures fall between the data provided by the TES and TPS, it is important to note that the BLS collects data from enterprises with less than 200 employees. Thus, large enterprises are under-represented in the sample. This suggests that a higher rather than a lower estimate of industry training is warranted by the ABS data overall. Estimates of the number of employees receiving training from their employers in the period of the survey suggest that 68 per cent received on-the-job training whilst 46 per cent received structured training. These figures are broadly in line with those of the SET for on-the-job training. The numbers receiving structured training are higher than the number receiving in-house training in the SET. However, the definition of structured training in the BLS is broader than that of in-house training courses in the SET.

In sum, it has been proposed that there may well be a higher level of training than has been acknowledged hitherto, particular that taking place in large Australian enterprises and when encompassing a wider set of criteria about learning –related activities in the workplace. This is important because it suggests an interest in, action by, engagement by employees and commitment to skill development by employers that provides a positive platform upon which to base policy. The TPS and the more recent TPES data indicate that there is interest and a willingness on the part of Australian enterprises to sponsor skill development. However, while the picture being painted may be more positive than anticipated, it is necessary to engage another kind of reality: that of comparisons with other countries, including those with whom we compete in the global marketplace

International comparisons

In recent years, data showing an apparent decline in training expenditure and in the hours of training provided to employees of Australian enterprises in the wake of the abolition of the Training Guarantee Scheme has led to charges that employers are reducing their commitment to training and that policies need to devised to compel them to increase their investments in training (Hall, Buchanan and Considine, 2002). Similar calls have also been heard the UK where employers have been blamed for that country's apparent poor record on employer training (Keep and Payne, 2002).

However, it is by no means clear that Australian employers spend so much less than many counterparts in other developed nations as is often implied. Figures from the European Union's Continuing Vocational Training Survey (CVTS II) show that Australia lies towards the top end of the normal range of employer training expenditure of about 0.5 to 1.7 per cent of payroll costs. Table 4 displays data from the most recent Training Expenditure and Practices Survey (ABS 2003) with data from CVTS II. Whilst not strictly comparable, the data are very consistent in that they measure the direct, net training costs borne by employers.

Table 4: Percentage of Wages and Salaries Spent by Employers on Employee Training: Australia (2002) and selected EU countries (1999).

Country	% payroll	Country	% payroll
Australia (2002)*	1.3	France	1.3
Denmark	1.7	Finland	1.3
Netherlands	1.7	Germany	0.9
Norway	1.6	Austria	0.8
Ireland	1.5	Spain	0.5

Source: All figures derived from the Eurostat CVTSII database except those marked with an asterisk.

*   Australian Bureau of Statistics, 2003*

Although these figures are only broadly comparable, it is nevertheless clear that assumptions that Australia lags well behind other developed nations in employer training expenditure are at least highly questionable and probably inaccurate. The data suggest that Australia lies towards the upper end of the normal range of employer expenditure on training of existing workers of between 0.5 and 1.7 per cent of payroll costs. It is interesting to note from these data that countries such as Germany that have been held up in the past as models for the Australian training system, fare less well when comparisons are based on the continuous training provided by employers than on the training provided for young people through the apprenticeship system. Also, the comparison with France with its well-known training levy system is most noteworthy.

In summary, it appears from the realities provided by different sets of data that a significant amount of training is being provided by Australian employers, and it may be higher than the current orthodoxy suggests. Some 80 per cent of Australian workers report receiving some form of training from their employers. Over 80 per cent of Australian employers claim to be providing some form of training for their employees. Between one third and one half of Australian workers are taking part in formal, structured training in the workplace with 70 per cent of workers taking part in on-the-job training. Over 40 per cent of Australian employers claim to provide structured training.

Why do enterprises train their employees?

In Australia, Smith and his colleagues have investigated the determinants of enterprise training (Smith and Hayton, 1999). Over a two-year period from 1994-1996, a research team from Charles Stuart University and the University of Technology, Sydney studied 42 organisations in depth and carried out a survey of 1750 studies of Australian private sector organisations.

Organisations in the following five industry sectors were studied:

- Building and Construction,

- Food Processing,

- Electronics Manufacturing,

- Retailing,

- Finance and Banking.

The research team developed a model of how training operates at the organisational level. The model is illustrated in Figure 1.

Figure 1: Model of Enterprise Training

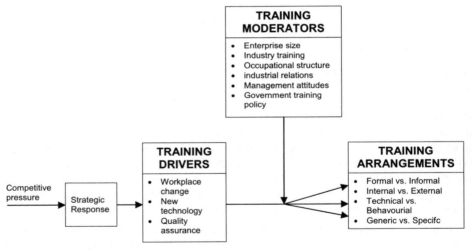

Source: Smith 1998

The research identified three key drivers of enterprise training.

- Workplace change: The extent and pace of workplace change varied between enterprises and between industries. This included the introduction of teamwork, new management practices and new forms of work organisation.

- Quality assurance: A particular form of workplace change that emerged as a consistently significant driver of enterprise training was quality improvement. However, the interpretation of quality improvement differed significantly across industries and between enterprises ranging from quality accreditation to the use of Total Quality Management (TQM).

- New technology: This included new product and process technology, although the extent of technological innovation was greater in the manufacturing and finance sectors than in construction or retail. New product technologies often involved on-the-job training for employees who would be producing the new product. Training for new process technology was more extensive.

The operation of the training drivers was moderated by a range of factors internal to the enterprise. The model of enterprise training identified the following six training moderators:

- Enterprise size,
- Industry traditions of training,
- Occupational structure,
- Industrial relations,
- Management attitudes,
- Government training policy.

The outcomes of the processes of interaction between drivers and moderators are the training arrangements that are finally put in place. The diversity of the arrangements in terms of the dimensions of training activity – formal versus informal, external versus internal, technical versus behavioural, generic versus specific – as well as the overall levels of expenditure on training and the distribution of that training between occupational groups in the workforce, is the product of the unique interactions between training drivers and training moderators that take place within each enterprise.

Following the work on the drivers of enterprise training, Smith and his colleagues examined the impact of workplace change on the type and extent of training provided by enterprises (Smith et al, 2003). This research involved a survey of 3,500 businesses investigating the links between different forms of workplace change and the type of training provided to employees. Five forms of workplace changes were investigated.

- Teamworking: The research examined both the extent of teamworking adopted in enterprises and the degree of autonomy given to teams. 63 per cent of responding enterprises reported that they used teamworking. However, the results also showed that the level of autonomy granted to teams was generally in the low-medium category. The incidence of high team autonomy was relatively uncommon. Thus, whilst teamworking appears to be an extensively adopted form of workplace change, most teams enjoy only a limited degree of autonomy.

  The adoption of teamworking resulted in a greater decentralisation of the training function, a higher level of workplace delivery of training and a more even distribution of training. Higher levels of team autonomy were associated with a greater use of external training provision and a greater formalisation of training.

- Total Quality Management: 43.7 per cent of responding enterprises reported a high level of commitment to some form of TQM. This was also associated with a greater level of decentralisation of training responsibility and a focus on generic skills. TQM was also associated with a greater use of internal training resources and provision of nationally accredited training.

- Lean production: 44.5 per cent of responding enterprises reported a high commitment to lean production techniques. This was associated with a reduction in training due to cost cutting measures, a more informal approach to training and less likelihood of training specialists existing in the enterprise.

- Learning Organisation: 40.2 per cent of respondents reported a high level of commitment to the principles of the learning organisation. This was associated a greater level of decentralisation of training, greater attention to the training of managers, a focus on generic skills in training and a greater use of coaching and mentoring.

- Business process re-engineering: 28.3 per cent of responding enterprises reported a high level of commitment to business process re-engineering. This resulted in a greater use of accredited training, a higher degree of workplace delivery of training and a more even distribution of training amongst different groups of employees.

This research appears to confirm the importance of workplace change in stimulating industry training but it is clear that the form of change adopted can have a significant impact on the type of training that occurs and who receives it. Other results to come from this research included the following:

- The relationship of training to business strategy: A key finding from the study was the importance of the link between training and business strategy as a driver of enterprise training. This link was positively correlated with almost all of the measures of training used in the study and appeared to be the single most important factor in boosting the incidence of industry training.

- The growing importance of generic or "soft" skills training: Enterprises appeared to be less concerned with training in the job-related technical skills but more with training in skills such as problem-solving, working with others and communication. These generic or transferable skills produce a degree of workforce flexibility and adaptability which is congruent with the importance of workplace change as a driver of industry training.

- The importance of the individual: Enterprises in the research were moving away from the "blanket" provision of training at the enterprise level and increasingly towards the notion that the individual employee must take responsibility for his/her own training. The role of the enterprise is to act as a broker in the relationship between individuals and a variety of training providers.

- Changing nature of training: All of the forms of workplace change adopted appeared to be reinforcing a flight away from the traditional training structures seen in Australian enterprises – training departments with training specialists and instructors. In many cases formal training departments had been abolished, responsibility for training had been devolved to line managers and training was delivered by a new breed of workplace instructors – employees whose primary responsibility was not training but had taken on a training role in addition to their other duties.

Many of these findings have been echoed in other studies of industry training in Australia. Analysis of the BLS (ABS, 1999) shows that across a range of measures the incidence of industry training is far higher in business that have adopted a formal strategic or business plan than in those that have no business plan. 86 per cent of enterprises with a business plan provided on-the-job training compared to 58 per cent of enterprises without a plan. 67 per cent of enterprises with a business plan provided structured training compared to only 34 per cent of businesses without a plan. Of all the measures contained in the BLS data the existence of a formal business or strategic plan is the one most strongly associated with a higher incidence of industry training.

A recent study commissioned by the Australian Industry Group (AIG) examined the future skills and training needs of Australian manufacturing industry (Allen Consulting Group, 2006). The study involved discussions with senior business leaders and a survey of 500 employers who are members of the AiG. The AiG study examined the reasons that their members trained their employees. The findings are presented in Table 4:

Table 4: Company Training Objectives in the Australian Industry Group

Reasons for training	% Enterprises agreeing
Improve our quality	96.0
Meet customer needs	92.0
Improve your competitiveness	89.0
Build commitment to the company	85.0
Support innovation	85.0
Implement workplace change	84.0

Source: Allen Consulting Group 2006

These reasons for training bear remarkable resemblance to the reasons for training adduced by the TPS. Although the implementation of workplace change ranks sixth in the AiG list of reasons for training, issues of quality improvement and supporting innovation attest to the overwhelming importance of workplace change in the factors that this group of Australian enterprises view as driving their training efforts.

The study also confirmed the importance of the link between training and business strategy in the plans of the enterprises in the survey. Seventy-four per cent of the AiG enterprises saw the inability to secure skilled staff as a major barrier to company success in the next three years. The AiG enterprises also emphasised the importance of training for generic skills citing basic skills such as literacy and numeracy, information technology capability, and relationship skills such as problem solving, communication and a willingness to learn as the "core" skills which they demand in new and existing employees.

The research points to a number of key factors that are associated with the provision of industry training in Australian enterprises:

Workplace change: Workplace change is a key factor in enterprises' decisions to change. The form of change varies but an emphasis on quality improvement and flexibility comes through most of the recent Australian research in this area. The introduction of new technology is also important but in conjunction with the development of new sets of skills, including multiskilling to make enterprises more competitive.

Generic skills: The evidence suggests strongly that enterprises have moved away from an emphasis on training for job-related technical skills and more towards skills that will introduce greater degrees of adaptability and flexibility in the workforces of Australian enterprises. Thus, the traditional human capital explanations for the provision of only enterprise "specific" training by employers seems to be breaking down quickly as enterprises become increasingly concerned with the provision of highly general and transferable skills, regardless of the dangers of poaching the external labour market.

Training and business strategy: All recent studies of industry training bear out the importance of the close connection between training and business strategy. There appears to be a growing realisation amongst enterprises that training and skills have an important part to play in their future competitiveness. The importance of this link appears to be born out empirically by research evidence which shows a strong association between increases in industry training and strong links to business strategy.

New training structures: At the same time as enterprises are taking a more strategic approach to their training, the organisation of training within enterprises is changing reflecting the management fashion for decentralisation and the vesting of higher levels of responsibility in both line managers and in individual workers.

Thus, specialist training departments are giving way to structures based on workplace instructors with an increasing emphasis on enterprises brokering training opportunities for individuals who take responsibility for meeting their own training needs.

What are Australian Industry's Future Training Needs?

It has been commonplace in recent years to refer to the upskilling effect of globalisation on developed economies. This argument proposes that globalisation is driven by the impact of new communications technologies which allow enterprises to compete in higher value added niche markets (Marginson, 2000). It has been argued by Reich and others that globalisation is leading to shifts in the skill profiles of occupations in developed countries, away from the production worker and towards the more highly skilled "symbolic analyst". In Australia, Maglen and Shah (1998) have traced the rise of the symbolic analyst in the labour market and argue that the skills requirements for jobs in the Australian labour market are increasing. There is some evidence from Australian enterprises that now supports this view. The AiG study and work by the Department of

Education, Training and Youth Affairs (DETYA, 2000) have shown that the traditional skills requirements of Australian industry are changing.

Most jobs in Australian Industry Group companies are expected to move up the skill ladder, reflecting the more sophisticated nature of production and service and the greater level of knowledge embodied in the work taking place among these companies. Eighty-five per cent of AiG companies saw building the skills base of their organisations as their second most important competitive strategy in the next three years (Allen Consulting Group, 2006, p.18). However, the future source of these higher level skills is in some doubt. The AiG study shows that recruitment of apprentices and trainees, the traditional means by which Australian enterprises have sought to meet their future skill requirements, is not likely to grow. This view has been supported by work carried out for the national review of skills shortages in the trades occupations co-ordinated by the federal Department of Education, Training and Youth Affairs (DETYA, 2000). This work has shown that across the traditional trades areas of electro-technology, mechanical/fabrication engineering and automotive repair the numbers of apprentices and trainees recruited by Australian enterprises has been declining since the early 1990s. In most of these trades areas, the decline has been arrested in the last two years with some trades, notably electro-technology showing strong growth in the numbers of apprentices recruited. However, these trades report significant skills shortages which are unlikely to be alleviated in the short-medium term through apprentice recruitment, with its long lead times to completion, or through the migration programme, a traditional source of skills for Australian industry. The reports from the three working parties, established to examine each of the trades' occupational areas, all emphasise the importance of re-skilling existing workers to meet the growing skills deficit. This has significant implications for the growth of employer sponsored industry training.

The importance of the re-training of existing workers has also been highlighted by work carried out by the National Centre for Vocational Education Research (NCVER) on the training needs of older workers (Smith, 1999). The NCVER work showed that the Australian population is rapidly ageing in line with international demographic trends. The median age of the Australian population, currently at 34 years, will increase to about 45 years by 2051. By this time over 25 per cent of the population will be aged over 65 years compared to 10 per cent in 1997. A key contributor to the greying of the population is the increasing health of older people. Advances in medical technology have led to a steady increase in the life expectancy for people, particularly in the developed world. For non-indigenous Australians, life expectancy at birth in 1996 was 81 years for females and 75 years for males. These rates are confidently expected to grow in coming years.

At the same time, the ageing of the population is being accompanied by a significant demographic "bust", with the lower birth rates of recent years contributing to a steep decline in the proportion of young people in the population aged 19-24 years.

The combination of more people living longer and a lowering proportion of young people in the population will have a significant impact on the age structure of the Australian workforce. As employers compete for a decreasing number of younger workers, they will be compelled to reconsider the role of older workers. The future skill needs of Australian industry will be increasingly met through training existing older workers already in the workforce rather than through the recruitment of younger people for training.

These rather optimistic views about the upward trajectory of Australian skill levels in the wake of globalisation and occupational change are tempered by work analysing the impact of labour market changes on the skills and training needs of Australian workers. The most important trends in the nature of work in Australia in recent years have been the growth in the numbers of casualised workers and the increasing incidence of outsourcing in Australian enterprises.

Using data from the Australian Bureau of Statistics and the Australian Workplace Industrial Relations Survey (Morehead et al, 1997), Vanden Heuvel and Wooden (1999) have shown that the proportion of casual workers has grown from 15.8 per cent of the workforce in 1984 to almost 27 per cent in 1998. The definition of "casual" workers is somewhat fraught, with a number of studies showing that casual workers may enjoy what amounts to permanent employment with a single employer. The ABS has defined casual workers as workers who do not enjoy employment benefits such as paid leave and sick leave and whose degree of attachment to the enterprise is thus lower than a permanent employee. This definition seems to capture the variety of employment arrangements found amongst casual workers whilst emphasising the precarious nature of their jobs. Vanden Heuvel and Wooden examined the experience of training for both casual and permanent employees. They gathered data on the incidence of in-house training, external training undertaken with employer support (employer pays for training) and external training unsupported by the employer (employee pays for the training). The results for 1997 are summarised in Table 6.

Table 6: Percentage of Permanent and Casual Employees Receiving Training 1997

Type of employee	% receiving in-house training	% receiving external training (employer supported)	% receiving external training (unsupported)
Permanent	40.5	15.3	9.0
Casual	16.7	3.4	13.2

Source: Vanden Heuvel and Wooden 1999

The data show clearly that casual employees are significantly disadvantaged in terms of employer sponsored training whether it is provided in-house or externally. This is not a surprising finding as employers may view casual employees as more likely to leave the enterprise as a result of their employment arrangements and therefore less worthy of investment. However, casual workers appear to undertake a significant amount of external training on their own account. This finding shows that although casual workers may not receive training from their employers to the same degree as their permanent colleagues, they are nevertheless investing in their own training and development. This supports the notion, discussed earlier, that workers are becoming more responsible for their own training and development and that training is becoming a more individualised process within Australian enterprises.

The degree of outsourcing in the Australian economy is more difficult to estimate. Vanden Heuvel and Wooden estimate that between 4 and 10 per cent of the workforce may be employed as contractors to other organisations. However, they caution that this figure may well understate the extent of outsourcing as many self-employed workers would not categorise themselves as contractors, and employees of labour hire firms may view themselves as permanently employed although they are involved in the contracting business. A survey of labour hire firms conducted by KPMG Management Consulting in Australia (KPMG, 1998) showed that the major reason for the use of outsourcing was to meet peak periods of demand for the enterprise. In many cases this involved the use of highly skilled labour (for maintenance tasks and so on), so it cannot be concluded that outsourcing involves only the use of low skilled workers. However, the incidence of training within labour hire firms appeared to be quite low. Only 14 per cent of labour hire forms in the survey responded that they employed an apprentice or trainee. The expectation appeared to be that employees were recruited for their existing skills and were expected to maintain those skills at their own expense and in their own time. The growth of outsourcing would seem to be associated with a decrease in the incidence of industry training as enterprises no longer carry the responsibility for the training of outsourced workers and labour hire forms place little importance in training their own staff.

This assumption may be challenged by the data from Vanden Heuvel and Wooden (1999) who show that outsourcing seems to be associated with an increase in the incidence of in-house training for employees and in the level of training expenditure. The data for these observations comes from the Australian Workplace Industry Relations Survey (AWIRS). Vanden Heuvel and Wooden cautioned that the measures of training used in the survey are crude with a large potential for error. However, the AWIRS data seems to suggest that outsourcing, whilst it may lead to a decrease in training for the employees whose functions are outsourced, does not appear to lead to a decrease in training for those who remain.

In summary, it appears that the skills and training requirements for Australian enterprises are changing. There appears to be an increasing demand in Australian industry for higher levels of skills and recognition that industry will have to inverse its training effort in order to secure these skills. Higher level skills are already in short supply in many traditional skilled occupations.

The source of these skills in the future will have to be the re-training of existing workers rather than the recruitment of people with the skills ready made. This shift towards adult re-skilling is also being driven by demographic projections which show that the Australian workforce is aging and that employers will increasingly rely on their older workers as sources of new skills in the future.

Changes in the Australian labour market are emphasising the emergence of non-standard forms of employment – casualised and outsourced workers. Although both of these trends are associated with a lower incidence of employer supported training, it is clear that both casual and outsourced workers depend on their skills for their employment and are increasingly undertaking training at their own expense to maintain and increase their skills. This goes hand in hand with the individualisation of industry training and a changing role for the enterprise as a broker rather than a provider of training.

Despite this apparent decrease in expenditure levels on industry training in recent years, there is considerable evidence to show that Australia is developing a culture of training and learning in its enterprises. 80 per cent of Australian workers receive some form of training in their workplace, over one third of workers receive structured training from their employer and over 60 per cent of enterprises provide structured training for their employees. These are high levels of industry training by world standards. This training effort is being driven by changes in the workplace and changes in the nature of work.

Change is endemic in Australian workplaces as it is in most countries in the developed world. It is the effort to capitalise on changes in the organisation of work and in new technologies in the workplace that are driving Australian enterprises to invest more in better training for their employees. But employers are not demanding the same skills as they did in the past. The evidence shows that it is generic and transferable skills, such as problem solving and teamwork that are in demand, together with higher levels of technical competence. These skills are no longer "specific" to the enterprise but are necessary to both the employer and the employee in the modern labour market. As a result, the traditional arrangements for industry training are giving way to new ones. Instead of enterprises providing highly specific job related training through blanket training programs devised for all employees, enterprises are decentralising the training role and providing more of a brokerage service to employees who take an increasing level of individual responsibility for their own training and development. It is, perhaps, this latter development that is the most critical for the future of industry training in Australia. Whilst an increasing number of casual and outsource workers are forced to invest in their own training to maintain their place in the labour market, individual responsibility for skills development is also passing to permanent employees in Australian enterprises. Meeting the fragmented demand created by this individualised training market is the future challenge for Australia's training system.

References

Allen Consulting Group (2006). *World class skills for world class industries.* Australian Industry Group, Melbourne.

Australian Bureau of Statistics (1990a). *Employer Training Expenditure Australia, July to September 1989.* AGPS, Canberra.

Australian Bureau of Statistics (1990b). *How Workers Get Their Training Australia, 1989.* AGPS, Canberra.

Australian Bureau of Statistics (1990c). *Projections of the Population of Australia, States and Territories, 1989 - 2031.* AGPS, Canberra.

Australian Bureau of Statistics (1991). *Employer Training Expenditure Australia, July to September 1990.* AGPS, Canberra.

Australian Bureau of Statistics (1994a). *Employer Training Expenditure Australia, July to September 1993.* AGPS, Canberra.

Australian Bureau of Statistics (1994b). *Training and Education Experience Australia, 1993.* AGPS, Canberra.

Australian Bureau of Statistics (1994c). *Employer Training Practices, Australia, 1994.* AGPS, Canberra.

Australian Bureau of Statistics (1997). *Employer Training Expenditure Australia, July to September 1996.* AGPS, Canberra.

Australian Bureau of Statistics (1998). *Employer Training Practices, Australia 1997.* AGPS, Canberra.

Australian Bureau of Statistics (1999). *Business Longitudinal Survey: Confidentialised Unit Record File.* AGPS, Canberra.

Australian Bureau of Statistics (2002). *Training and Education Experience Australia, 2001.* Australia, AGPS, Canberra.

Australian Bureau of Statistics (2003). *Employer Training Expenditure and Practices, 2001-02..* Australia, AGPS, Canberra.

Coopers & Lybrand (1994), *The Economic dimensions of education and training in the member states of the European Union.* - http://www.transcend.co.uk/eyll/ideas.htm.

Cully, M. and Richardson, S. (2002). *Employers' contributions to training: how does Australia compare with overseas?* National Institute of Labour Studies, Adelaide.

Department of Education, Training and Youth Affairs (2000).

Hall, R., Buchanan, J. and Considine, G. (2002). *'You value what you pay for': enhancing employers' contributions to skill formation and use: a discussion paper for the Dusseldorp Skills Forum Sydney*: Dusseldorp Skills Forum, Sydney.

Finegold, D. and Soskice, D. (1988). *The failure of British training: analysis and prescription.* Oxford review of economic policy, 4, 21-53.

Keep, E. and Payne, J. (2002). *Policy interventions for a vibrant work-based route - or when policy hits reality's fan (again)* in Evans, K., Hodkinson, P. and Unwin, L.: *Working to learn: transforming learning in the workplace* Kogan Page, London.

Kempnich, B., Butler, E. & Billett, S. (1999) *Irreconcilable Differences: Women in Small Business and Vocational Education and Training,* Leabrook, NCVER.

KPMG (1998). *Impact of the growth of labour hire companies on the apprenticeship system.* ANTA, Brisbane.

Maglen, L. & Shah, C. (1999). *Emerging Occupational Patterns in Australia in the Era of Globalisation and Rapid Technological Change: Implications for Education and Training.* Monash University-ACER Centre for the Economics of Education and Training, Melbourne.

Marginson, S. (2000). *The Changing Nature and Organisation of Work, and the Implications for Vocational Education and Training in Australia:* Issues paper. NCVER, Adelaide.

Morehead, A., Steele, M., Alexander, M., Stephen, K. & Duffin, L. (1997). *Changes at Work: the 1995 Australian Workplace Industrial Relations Survey (AWIRS 95).* Longman, Melbourne.

National Centre for Vocational Education Research (NCVER) (2002). *Australian Vocational Education and Training Statistics 2001: At a Glance,* NCVER, Adelaide.

Smith, A. (Ed) (1999). *Creating a Future: Training, Learning and the Older Person.* NCVER, Adelaide.

Smith, A. and Hayton, G. (1999). *What Drives Enterprise Training?   Evidence from Australia.* International Journal of Human Resource Management, 10:2. 251-272.

Smith, A., Noble, C., Oczkowski, E. & Macklin, R. (2003). *New Management Practices and Enterprise Training in Australia.* International Journal of Manpower, 24:1, 31-47.

Teicher, J. (1995). *The Training Guarantee: A Good Idea Gone Wrong.* in F. Ferrier & C. Selby-Smith (eds), *The Economics of Education and Training 1995*, AGPS, Canberra.

VandenHeuvel, A. & Wooden, M. (1999). *Casualisation and Outsourcing: Trends and Implications for Work-Related Training.* NCVER, Adelaide.

Can We Link and Match Training in the "Dual System" with Competency-Based Education and Training (CBET)?

A Discussion Note

Gert Loose

CBET and "Dual Training": Are they Comparable?

Christopher Dougherty's (Dougherty 1989) comprehensive 1989 World Bank study on training systems in developing countries categorized training systems into two groups – enterprise-based versus school-based. One year later George Psacharopoulos (Psacharopoulos 1990) examined the question "Why Educational Policies Can Fail" and came to the conclusion that "the substance of a (educational) policy should be based on a *research-proven cause and effect* relationship..." (p. 21). Previously, as early as 1972 Haccoun and Campbell (Haccoun, Campbell 1972) had provided empirical proof that lack of extra-functional skills such as "getting along with supervisors and fellow-workers" is the cause of the majority of cases of workers being released from their contracts. It is apparent from these findings that workplace success is substantially dependent on aspects of worker behaviour which cannot readily be acquired in school-based training, but require the incorporation of the workplace as a learning environment.

A World Bank Policy Paper on Vocational Technical Education and Training (World Bank 1991) strongly advocated "enterprise-based training" as "best practice". Yet the rise of the total systems version of competency-based training challenged the supremacy of enterprise-based training. The most common mode of enterprise-based training, the apprenticeship system, came under particular pressure. This system is often referred to as the "Dual System" of training since it attempts to go beyond training in the enterprise by encompassing the school as the second learning environment (therefore: "dual").

In contrast to the "Dual System" as a network of training which encompasses two learning environments, the CBET approach focuses on the definition of a differentiated system of skills which is in most cases externally assessed in order to verify required competencies in an objective way. This movement started in England and Wales with the creation of the 5-level system of National Vocational Qualifications (NVQs). Originally, NVQs were primarily introduced to offer formal recognition (through certification) of the skills of workers who had considerable experience on the job but lacked a formal certification. They were in particular used to document the skill level which the workers had achieved. Finally, in the absence of a consistent national system for categorizing qualifications in England and Wales, NVQs also proved to be a valuable tool for categorizing training programmes (cf. Eraut 1994).

Within a couple of years this approach became very popular in most Commonwealth nations and was increasingly promoted as "best practice" for introduction in developing countries. This overlooked the fact that developing countries were often in desperate need of the creation of an *effective training system*, i.e. of the development of training programmes and curricula. CBET on the other hand provided the *definition of competencies and the methodology for assessing them*; but it *failed* to provide the "T" in CBET, a learning process as the basis for the creation of *training* itself.

Nonetheless the clear and "comprehensible" structure of the CBET systems made them very popular with decision-makers in developing countries – in particular because this approach held out the promise of measuring objectively the outcome from the training systems that the decision-makers were in charge of (without being convinced themselves of their effectiveness). Furthermore, compared to the clear structure of CBET, it is difficult to make explicit the complex interdependencies which seem to be responsible for the apparent success of the dual system of training. Without deep educational, socio-psychological and socio-political insight, the advantages of the dual system of training remain "blurred". And even when the full potential of this system for effective training is recognized, the final reaction of decision-makers very often is: "Excellent, yet it cannot be done in our country."

Therefore, in the second half of the nineties, CBET and the Dual Training System have been seen as the two worldwide competing modes of training; but while CBET seemed to sweep from success to success and from one country to another, there was only limited evidence of the acceptability of (and support for) the dual system of training.

What is different today?

Three crucial developments have occurred:

First: Analysis of the basic traits of the CBET approach has revealed serious shortcomings in its application in directing instructional processes.

Second: The implications of increasing complexity and accelerated technological change in the workplace have become so dramatic that they increasingly render the CBET approach obsolete. CBET because of its internal logic focuses on "work"; but it cannot follow the incorporation of ongoing change in a "work-process orientation" of training which has become mandatory today.

Third: It has become evident that it is inappropriate to compare CBET with the Dual System of Training because CBET is an *approach*, while Dual Training refers to a *total system* of training. The approach underlying Dual Training should be termed Experience-Based Education and Training (EBET). EBET is work-process oriented while CEBT is assessment-oriented.

It is the intention of this paper to further detail these developments.

Figure 1: The Process and Outcome of Training

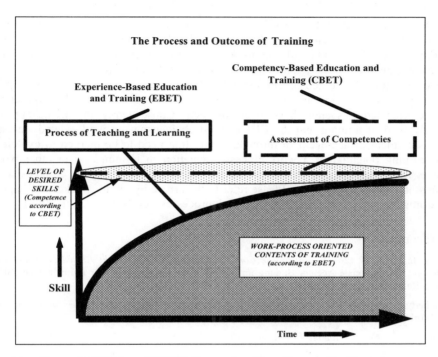

Reaching Beyond CBET and EBET Towards a New Concept in Training

Regardless of its shortcomings, the indisputable merit of CBET is that it has been based on standards which clearly focused on the actual *work* which had to be performed at the workplace. This positioned the purpose of training, (i.e. developing the ability to skilfully perform set work), in the center of the micro-level in human resource planning.

Because this perspective of providing a detailed account of the skills needed to perform the intended work was largely ignored by the dual system of training, dual training earned the criticism that the success of its programmes could evidently only be measured in terms of elapsed time for training.

On the other hand the scope of CBET did not encompass the dimension and the value of experience in training. In theory, the description of the standards did not predetermine the mode of training which would be employed in the programmes. In practice, however, the knowledge about the parameters of efficient training was exactly what was missing. Ultimately therefore CBET relied on "standards" which were the expected outcomes of the training programmes; but it did not provide the necessary guidance on how to organize the "training" as promised in its name.

In conclusion, CBET created an awareness of the need for standards while EBET emphasised the importance of actual experience in training. Consequently, up to the present day CBET lacks a refined pedagogical operationalisation of its approach, while EBET lacks instruments to prove the effectiveness of its programmes.

The increasing complexity of work and the work environment, and rapid advances in technology, have resulted in an unprecedented level of change and uncertainty in the workplace, which has to be reflected in skill requirements. It no longer seems feasible to focus on specific "work"; instead, work increasingly dissolves into generic "work processes" (cf. Tissot 2004). On the other hand, mere reliance on an appropriate learning environment in training can no longer give the assurance that the requirements of the knowledge society have been fulfilled. Consequently the EBET-approach underlying dual training and the CBET-approach focusing on work-related standards and assessment of achievement through skill-testing need to be merged to exploit the full learning potential of a work-process-orientation in training. Or in other words: Successful performance at today's workplace has to rely on mastering complexity and change in "work processes." – Please refer to the article by Spöttl/ Becker in Chapter 3 regarding the procedure for identifying work processes[1] (cf. Blings/ Spöttl 2003).

References

Blings, J.; Spöttl, G. (2003): *A European Core Occupational Profile for the Closed Loop and Waste Economy*. Ed.: Nationale Agentur Bildung für Europa at the Bundesinstitut für Berufsbildung (BIBB). Impuls-Reihe, Heft No. 9. Bonn

Dougherty, Ch. (1989). *The Cost-Effectiveness of National Training Systems in Developing Countries*. The World Bank. Washington D.C.

Eraut, M. (1994): *Developing Professional Knowledge and Competence*. Falmer Presse: London-Philadelphia.

Haccoun, R.R.; Campbell, R.E. (1972). *Training Methods and Intervention Strategies Relevant for Work Entry Problems of Youth*. Columbus Ohio: CVTE, The Ohio State University.

OSSTC (ed.) (2005). *Conducting a Work Process Analysis*. Ministry of Manpower. Muscat. Oman.

Psacharopoulos, G. (1990). *Why Educational Policies Can Fail*. World Bank Discussion Paper No. 82. Washington D.C.

Tissot, P. (2006): *Terminology of Vocational Training Policy A Multilingual Glossary for an Enlarged Europe*. Cedefop. http:// europass.cedefop.eu.int/img/dynamic/c313/cv1_en_US_glossary_4030_6k.pdf

Vocational and Technical Education and Training (1991). A World Bank Policy Paper. The World Bank. Washington D.C.

---

1   For the procedure of identifying core work processes see also the work at the Ministry of Manpower in the Sultanate of Oman (OSSTC 2005).

Chapter 3: The Malaysian Way to Support the Private Sector with Trained People

This chapter is targeting recent reform initiatives of the training sector in Malaysia. In many ways it is the core of this publication. The first article clearly reveals the huge challenges for Malaysia to respond competently to the requirements of the knowledge economy in particular with regard to the development of human resources. Malaysia is determined to make a decisive contribution to the value chain and to do a convincing development step towards becoming a fully industrialised society.

In the following articles the different perspectives of reform are elaborated, starting from the government policies on human resources development which provide the link to the intention of UNESCO's Youth Employment Network. Further on private-sector involvement is emphasized as an essential trait for the delivery of quality training and the challenge which this generates for training and education institutions is discussed in detail.

The second article reflects which challenges can be matched with the assistance of experience-based training and how the private sector should be integrated in this endeavour.

And finally the third article elaborates on the work-process analysis as the core instrument for understanding the skill requirements for the k-worker. Increasing complexity at the workplace and rapid technological changes make it necessary to "hang in" with the changing work process. Therefore the work-process analysis is the key for designing a qualification concept for the modern workplace.

Malaysian Government Policies on Human Resources Development: Towards Meeting the Needs of the Knowledge-Based Economy

Zanifa Md. Zain

Introduction

The past three decades have seen remarkable growth and development in the Malaysian economy. We now face a new challenge in how to react to the needs of the emerging knowledge economy and in particular how to develop the human resources a knowledge economy requires.

This short chapter will look at the past economic development and examine Malaysian Government policies on human resources development towards meeting the needs of a knowledge-based economy. This will include the evolution of policy and the rationale for Malaysia to shift to a knowledge-based economy.

Policy Evolution

Malaysian development policies can be classified into four major phases. The first was the period before the New Economic Policy (NEP), from 1957-70. The emphasis was on a "laissez faire" policy and economic and rural development. In 1971, the Government launched the New Economic Policy (NEP) with a two-prong strategy of poverty eradication and restructuring of society. The NEP was implemented through the First Outline Perspective Plan (OPP1), which covered the period 1971-1990. The main development thrust of the NEP was "Growth with Equity". The National Development Policy (NDP) was launched under the Second Outline Perspective Plan (OPP2) in the period between 1991-2000 and the main thrust was on "Balanced Growth". In 2001, the National Vision Policy (NVP) was launched. The thrust of the NVP is "Building a Resilient and Competitive Nation". Since 1991, all the development plans have been guided by the Vision 2020, which covers a thirty-year period from 1991-2020 and focuses on "Total Development".

There are seven major goals for the National Vision Policy. They are:

- Building a resilient nation by raising the quality of life as well as increasing economic resilience,

- Promoting an equitable society,

- Sustaining high economic growth,

- Enhancing competitiveness to meet the challenges of globalization and liberalization,

- Developing a knowledge-based economy as a strategic move to raise the value added of all economic sectors and optimizing the brain power of the nation,

- Strengthening human resource development to produce a competent, productive and knowledgeable workforce,

- Pursuing environmentally sustainable development to reinforce long-term rowth.

The central aims for the Human Resource Policy were laid down in the Third Outline Perspective Plan (2001-2010) and The Eighth Malaysia Plan (2001-2005) to meet the needs of a knowledge-based economy. These will be examined in more depth below.

The Malaysian Economy

The Malaysian economy underwent a deep structural transformation from an agriculture based, labour-driven economy during the 1960s to an industrial economy based on labour-intensive assembly production during the 1970s. During the 1980s, the manufacturing sector continued to expand with the development of heavy industries and import substitution industries. The Government embarked on public sector investment in heavy manufacturing industries such as automobiles, cement and iron and steel (see Figure 1).

Figure 1: Phases of Growth

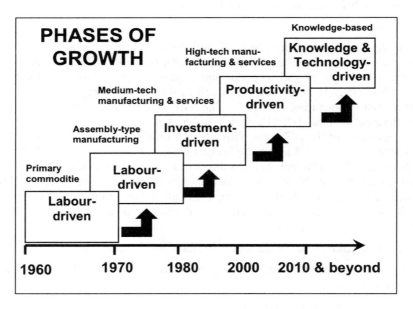

Until the mid-1990s Malaysia depended largely on capital investment to spearhead economic growth. Realizing that there are limitations to sustaining high levels of investment to support high growth, the focus shifted from an investment-driven strategy to a productivity-driven strategy and towards more capital and technology intensive activities, in both the manufacturing and service sectors. This shift began during the 7th Malaysia Plan.

However, globalization, liberalization and the rapid development of ICT have fundamentally changed the rules and nature of global trade and the flow of resources and competition. Malaysia's economy will now be knowledge and technology driven or a knowledge-based economy.

Malaysia has enjoyed a good track record of economic performance; the last decade has seen an average economic growth rate of 7.0 per cent. However, this economic growth has been based mainly on the input of capital and labour. The move towards a knowledge-based economy will require productivity driven growth. Greater emphasis therefore will be placed on building Malaysia's human capital and enhancing productivity and capacity for knowledge absorption and utilization.

For the 8th Malaysia Plan, the economy is projected to grow at an average rate of 7.5 per cent per annum with low inflation and an unemployment rate of 2.7 per cent. Per capita income has increased from Ringgit Malaysian (RM) 1,132 in 1970 to RM 13,359 in 2002 (US $ 1 = app. RM 3.40) and increased further up to 2006.

The rapid economic growth has been accompanied by profound changes in the structure of production. The contribution of agriculture to Gross Domestic Production (GDP) decreased to 8.7 per cent in 2000 while the manufacturing and services sectors increased to 33.4 per cent and 48 per cent respectively. In the knowledge-based economy, manufacturing and services will continue to be the leading growth sectors.

The Rationale for the Shift to a Knowledge-Based Economy

There are a number of underpinning reasons behind the planned move to a knowledge-based economy.

The first is that knowledge is seen as the next driver of economic growth and the move is central to sustaining the 7 per cent average annual growth foreseen in Vision 2020. Knowledge based activities will be a source of new economic growth, particularly in manufacturing and services.

The second rationale is to move up the value chain. Value added from pure production is declining, whilst product and process development, and activities such as packaging and marketing, have higher added value. Positioning Malaysia as a knowledge-based economy means to put more added value to its goods. This in turn entails a vigorous sectoral transformation within the value chain.

Eight major variables have been identified as critical indicators of added value to ensure Malaysia's elevation from what it is today to a level that it wants to be, as a knowledge-based economy. These variables are research and development, technology and process creation, product development and design, production, packaging, marketing, distribution and after sales support.

Although in comparative studies Malaysia is relatively strong in production, it employs relatively low levels of technology. Thus, at the global level, it remains less competitive. This is further aggravated by the limited added value both downstream and upstream of the production process after sales support and research and development. Therefore, it is imperative that knowledge utilisation is intensified at all stages of the value chain to ensure that Malaysia will attain its aspiration to become a knowledge-based economy. A knowledge-based economy with skilled human resources and an improved capacity for research and development will support the transition to high added value production.

The third rationale behind the transition to a knowledge based economy is the need to absorb new knowledge within the production process. Although the rate of change varies from one product to another, the last twenty years have seen a general trend of increasing trade in high and medium technology products as opposed to resource-based products and a decrease in trade in low technology products. It is also notable that there is an increasingly high technology input into resource based products.

The move to a knowledge-based economy is seen as fundamental to sustaining competitiveness. Malaysia is a small, open economy and needs to respond to global trends such as the adoption of ICT and the increase in knowledge intensity. The threatened loss of markets to low-wage developing economies has to be countered by increased competition with the advanced economies in high-technology industries (see Figure 2).

Figure 2: Positioning in the Value Chain with a Knowledge-Based Economy

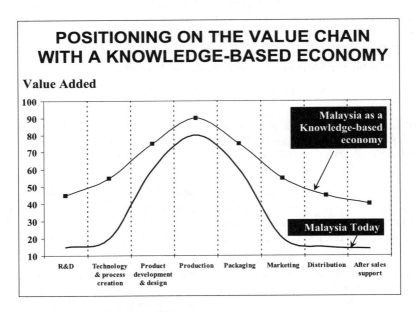

Features of a Knowledge-Based Economy

In a knowledge-based economy growth is premised on the acquisition, utilization and dissemination of knowledge. Existing industries will become more knowledge-intensive while new knowledge-based and enabling industries will emerge. The economy will be characterised by a higher contribution of knowledge-based activities and high-technology industries to employment, GDP and exports.

There will also be changes in the pattern of demand for manpower. This will include a demand for new skills and expertise including ICT skills. There will be increased demand for scientists and engineers in research and development. There will be a more general requirement for increased flexibility and for multi-skilled workers to meet changing occupational structures.

One of the main pre-requisites to support a knowledge-based economy is higher levels of education and training. It has been estimated that economies have to be able to at least double the rate of absorption of knowledge to enable sustainable growth and competitiveness. In 2005, the proportion of the labour force with tertiary level education was 20 per cent. This will need to increase to support the manpower requirements of the knowledge-based economy. The target is for 35 per cent of the work force to be educated to tertiary level by the end of 2010. This will require increased public investment in education. In 1996 public investment in education in Malaysia was 5.2 per cent of GDP, a low figure compared to other advanced economies. In 2005, however, 23 per cent of the public expenditure were invested in education.

Human Resource Policies

The main aim for human resource development in the Third Outline Perspective Plan (OPP3) was to develop a dynamic labour force that is capable of meeting the challenges of a knowledge economy in order to enhance the productivity and competitiveness of the economy.

Accessibility to quality education and training will be increased and efforts will be made to ensure that the education and training system has the capacity to enhance the quality of intellectual capital, as well as strengthening and expanding the human resource base (see Figure 3).

Globalization and rapid technological advances will intensify demand for highly skilled workers. Therefore existing education and training institutions will be expanded and upgraded and new institutions established.

To support the manpower requirements of the knowledge-based economy, a larger proportion of the labour force will need to have a higher level of educational attainment, especially at the tertiary level. Therefore, tertiary education will be expanded to achieve 40 per cent of participation for the 17-23 year old age cohort.

To develop universities as centres for the creation of intellectual capital and new knowledge, the curriculum and degree programmes of universities will be reviewed to ensure they are market-driven, anticipatory of future trends and facilitate the adoption of new technologies. Universities will be encouraged to forge closer collaboration and partnerships with industry for research and training. The private sector is being encouraged to play a bigger role in the provision of education and training especially in multidisciplinary knowledge areas and in new disciplines such as biotechnology and bioinformatics. To meet the increasing demand for highly skilled workers for more complex production processes, more advanced skills training centres in specialized fields will be established.

Access to education will be increased through the construction of centralized schools in remote areas together with improvements in the education infrastructure and the training of teachers. The Government will also establish community colleges to provide hands-on training for early school leavers and for workers.

The private sector is being encouraged to increase their involvement at all educational levels. At the tertiary level, they are encouraged to establish new, purpose-built campuses. The role of the private sector is seen as particularly vital in the provision of technical and industrial courses. Hence, the Skills Development Fund will be expanded to include trainees in private training institutions.

Figure 3: Absorbing Knowledge

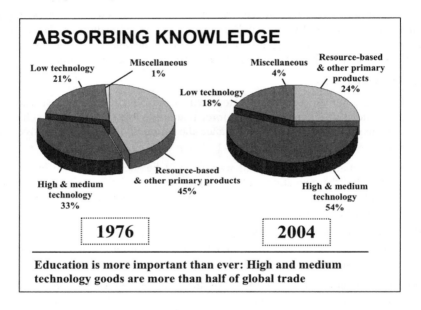

Strategies to create excellence in the education and training system will be directed towards nurturing creative thinking and learning skills particularly in primary and secondary schools. Therefore the school curriculum will be reviewed to generate creativity and independent learning among students as well as incorporate new aspects of knowledge and technology and more innovative teaching methods.

The student-centred learning approach will be strengthened along with more use of computer-based resources and multimedia technology for teaching. A centre to nurture innovation and creativity for students with special talents and abilities will also be set up.

Training and retraining is seen as the critical enabler in equipping the future workforce with suitable skills and facilitating the present workforce in adjusting to a knowledge-economy. To ensure that training programmes meet the requirements of the economy, the curriculum and teaching materials will be standardised for quality training. More training will be given by training institutions in soft skills such as communications, management and problem solving. The new programmes will focus on the development of social and learning competencies in skill training institutions and will strengthen the academic foundations of trainees in Science, Mathematics and English language.

Training institutions will be encouraged to adopt the dual training approach through apprenticeship schemes and to strengthen the delivery system through the use of ICT and web-based learning. The instructor training programmes will be expanded, especially in new technologies, in order to increase the supply of qualified instructors with the provision of special incentives to attract and retain instructors with industrial experience.

The promotion of lifelong learning is seen as critical to developing a knowledge-seeking culture in Malaysia and to enhancing productivity and employability. Therefore the government will promote and initiate programmes for lifelong learning. This will include the following measures:

- The provision of affordable access to training courses and education programmes through the internet or other ICT-related media,

- The provision of more diversified distance learning programmes to cater for different levels of educational attainment and interest,

- The establishment of community colleges, open universities and distance education to provide access to tertiary education and skills upgrading,

- An increase in support services through public libraries,

- Employers will be encouraged to promote lifelong learning through training and retraining to equip workers with new skills and knowledge.

To increase the supply of local labour, efforts will be made to increase the participation rate of women in the labour force by setting up kindergartens and ensuring better access to training opportunities. New modes of working including teleworking and part time employment will be encouraged to provide flexibility for working for women. It is also intended to attempt to reduce the dependence on foreign workers.

Malaysia requires a pool of scientific and technical manpower to leverage new knowledge and technological advancements to achieve sustainable growth. Therefore, scientific and technical education and training programmes will be expanded, and enrolment increased, to achieve a 60:40 ratio of Science to Arts students in order to create a critical mass of scientific and technical personnel.

Enrolment in scientific and technical degree programmes in local tertiary institutions, especially at post-graduate levels, will be expanded and the provision of scholarships for post graduate and post-doctoral studies as well as fellowships for graduate research will be increased. Local research and development capacity will be enhanced through joint activities between universities and industry as well as between Malaysians and researchers from other countries. In this respect the "brain-gain" programme will be expanded to attract both foreign scientific and technical personnel and Malaysian scientists and technologists who are working abroad to go back to Malaysia on a short and long term basis.

Through these different measures, it was predicted that the ratio of scientific and technical scientists and technologists will increase from 10 per 10,000 of the labour force in 2000 to 30 per 10,000 by 2005. This figure was reached and is still relevant.

It is critical that wage increases are commensurate with increases in productivity so that the competitiveness of the economy is further enhanced. The adoption of the guidelines for a Productivity-Linked Wage System (PLWS) established in 1996 and was intensified through seminars, workshops and company visits in the subsequent years. The online network database on productivity benchmarking in the manufacturing and agriculture sectors will be expanded to include other sectors.

The effective distribution and dissemination of labour market information will enable the flexible and efficient functioning of the labour market in response to changing market needs. Towards this end the implementation of an electronic labour exchange with fully integrated, coherent and dynamic labour market information system will be accelerated.

In line with the objective of establishing Malaysia as a regional centre of education excellence, local universities will be encouraged to develop centres of excellence. Greater autonomy and flexibility will be given to public universities to strengthen their research and development capacity. Universities will be encouraged to promote programmes abroad to attract an influx of foreign students and efforts will be made to attract reputable foreign universities to set up campuses in Malaysia, especially for the provision of science and technology courses and for undertaking research.

Inculcating positive values and attitudes among Malaysians will be crucial in increasing and sustaining productivity and enhancing competitiveness. Measures to promote positive values and attitude include the reintroduction of civics education in the curriculum for moral or religious education in schools and the implementation of a code of work ethics at the workplace. Among corporate and business organisations, tenets of positive corporate governance and professional practice will be promoted.

This effort will be complemented by the family unit and the community through intensifying the implementation of motivational and attitudinal-based family and society-oriented programmes.

The shift to knowledge-based economy will spawn new areas of economic activities which entail a change in the pattern of demand for manpower. High technology and science-based industries as well as knowledge-intensive industries such as pharmaceutical and research and development activities will generate new jobs requiring tertiary education. The fastest growing occupations, which will account for 32.2 per cent of new jobs during the period, will be in the professional and technical occupations and in administration and management.

It is estimated that the economy will require 137,200 more engineers and 331,700 more engineering assistants, as well as increased numbers of ICT personnel within the next 10 years.

Conclusion

In this short paper we have attempted to explain the rationale for a policy orientation towards the knowledge economy. The development of a knowledge based economy will have profound repercussions for the structure and patterns of employment and skills and knowledge requirements in Malaysia. This in turn will require major changes and developments in the education and training system and the development of a new culture and infrastructure to support lifelong learning in the community and in the workplace.

Experience-Based Training for Malaysia: Private-Sector Involvement in Training K-Workers[1]

Gert Loose; Abdul Hakim Juri

Introduction

The quest for success in global competition incorporates the quest for the best approach in optimizing the productivity of a nation's workforce. Australia and Germany are both world renowned for their conceptual contributions in this field. The respective articles in this book have presented an insight into the rich experience in training of both countries. Interestingly, the experience of both these lead countries highlights the indispensable role of the private sector in quality training. This has been broken down even further to the government perspective, to industry level, and to the company level of Siemens, in other articles in this book.

What is Malaysia's role in this global competition? Where do we stand and what are our options for the future? "Malaysia boleh" in training is our challenge to excel in the design of our training approach and develop it truly within the Malaysian culture. This article attempts to present the outline for this development process.

Human Resource Development as a National Priority: Maintaining Malaysia's Competitive Edge in the Global Market

We are living in a global economic and business culture; most of our concerns regarding security, the environment and the future at large are influenced by variables on this scale. The position of each national workforce in the global market has become the prime point of reference for the development of effective policies in training.

In its "Programme for the First Decade of the New Millennium", UNESCO describes the dominance of global issues regarding human resource development in the following way:

- Globalization has created a new international agenda for development.

- The preparation of a productive, flexible labour force is crucial to (global) competition in the twenty-first century (UNESCO 1999).

---

1 With the assistance of Stefan Erber, Fadzliah Kamaruddin and Oliver Haas.

These global concerns have been met by Malaysia's national development policies in the following ways:

- Growth in productivity is recognized as the main constituent of national development.

- Human resource development is considered to be the core area of concern for national development.

- Training has become a national priority (Ninth Malaysia Plan 2006).

Basic economic statistics illustrate the close interlinkage between global and national dimensions. Huge multinational companies outperform whole countries. The Exxon Mobil Company had a total revenue worldwide of $US Bn291.3 (Fortune 2006) in 2004, in comparison to GNIs of $US Bn82.5 for New Zealand and $US Bn117.1 for Malaysia (World Bank 2006).

Any national action taken has to reflect the global perspective which constitutes the background of operation for multinational companies. It is in this context that Malaysia's performance as an exporting nation is outstanding. In the year 2004, Malaysia held the 18th rank with respect to worth of exports worldwide among the main exporting nations (World Trade Organisation 2004), shortly behind Spain and in front of Saudi Arabia. Based on a per capita comparison between the top seventeen exporting countries, Malaysia would rank 10th.

The credit for this achievement must be given to the Malaysian workforce. Yet, it is not the right time to celebrate. We are threatened with losing this competitive edge over other countries. The increase in wages (2.8 %) has outgrown the increase in productivity (-0.4 %, from 2000 to 2001) (Department of Statistics Malaysia 2001). This trend must be broken and human resource development is integral in this context. Jerome Bruner (Bruner 1972) has proposed that any complexity we encounter can be broken down into information that is conveyable. The impact of quality training on productivity in the light of national development is one such complexity, providing a baseline mark to be focused on. The Malaysian national development plans (3rd Outline Perspective Plan, 9th Malaysia Plan and 2nd Industrial Master Plan) provide the framework for appraising these issues. The Third Outline Perspective Plan e.g. states: "Among the characteristics of a knowledge-based economy is a highly skilled labour force ... Skills and knowledge become the main assets for the economy to gain competitiveness." (The Third Outline Perspective Plan 2001-2010).

The criteria for today's human resource development emphasise the fundamental role of the knowledge worker (k-worker)[2] in the design of training. This serves as an orientation mark in our quest to identify Malaysia's concept for training, pushing this development towards "Vision 2020" (Sarji 1997). In reviewing processes of change in organizational development in high-tech companies, we realize that the k-worker has

---

2   The term "knowledge worker" (k-worker) is often wrongly applied for workers who are dependent on computers in their work. A meaningful definition should refer to the k-worker as an individual who has to rely on his or her cognitive capabilities to self direct action at the workplace.

become one of the prime agents for change in today's high-tech work environment. It is the core issue of this chapter to define the central qualification requirements that characterize the training of k-workers.

Orientation Marks for Training K-Workers

According to a very brief and pragmatic definition, "training" can be perceived as "preparation for performance at the workplace". In the identification of competencies (skills) needed at the workplace, the sweeping success of the DACUM[3] approach has brought an end to the time consuming and sometimes diffuse procedures of seeking expert advice in the development of training programmes. The transparent format for its structured interview with members of the "target occupation" for the development of a training programme has made curriculum development a clear and simple process. The DACUM process expresses "competence" as the core element of competency-based training.

There has been an ongoing discussion about the merits and shortcomings of competency-based training (Kerka n.y.), but it has been due to dramatic changes at the workplace itself that the validity and feasibility of defining a sequence of skills as a benchmark level for determining vocational competence has been brought into question. Two phenomena, the steadily increasing complexity of work situations and the accelerated pace of technological change in high-tech areas, have severely shortened the reasonable "longevity" of relevant skills which is indispensable for competency-based training. Therefore, it is crucial to analyze the impact which both phenomena have on the training needs at the workplace (cf. Markowitsch 2002).

Phenomenon 1: Steadily Increasing Complexity at the Workplace

The complexity of most work situations in industry is steeply increasing. From laundry machines to photocopiers, to cars, a host of technological options are incorporated into existing technical solutions. If, for example, the total number of pages of all repair manuals which exist for a particular brand of car are counted, it becomes evident that in particular the nineties have witnessed a dramatic increase in the volume of these manuals. This reflects the exorbitant increase in the complexity of car repair; whereas it took 202 pages to describe the necessary repairs of the Opel 1.2 litre in 1933, it takes 13,866 pages to understand all potential repair of the Opel Omega B in 1998 (see Figure 1).

Still, it is the car mechanic to whom we entrust the repair, in 1933 as well as today. What is the impact of this boundless complexity on the design of his training programme? It seems doubtful that competency-based training can cope with this pace of change.

---

3   DACUM = Develop a Curriculum. Robert E. Norton, Dacum Handbook 2nd ed. Columbus, OH: CTE, Ohio State University, 1997.

Figure 1: Steadily Increasing Complexity at the Workplace.

Phenomenon I: Steadily Increasing Complexity at the Workplace

An Illustration:
The Total Number of Pages of
the Repair Manuals for Opel
Cars from 1933 to 1998

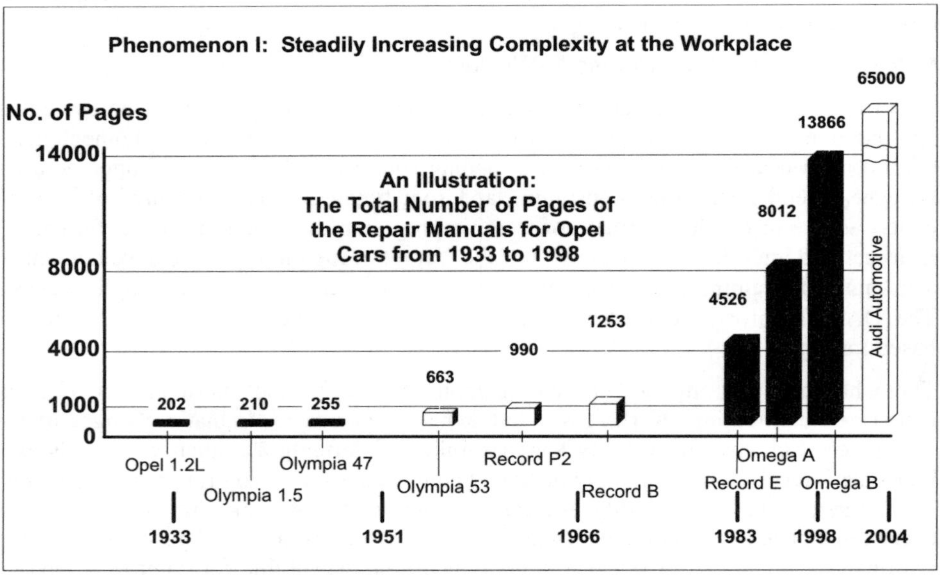

Source: Spöttl; Teggemann 1999, 2001, 2004

Phenomenon 2: The Accelerated Pace of Technological Change:

In order to explain the effect of change on the established knowledge in a particular field of technology, the concept of the "half life" of radiating material has been borrowed from nuclear physics. The half life of radiating material states how much time will pass until half of the isotopes have lost their radiation, and are no longer useful for their intended purpose. Correspondingly the half life of knowledge states how much time will pass until half of the knowledge which is needed to be in command of a particular area of technology (such as car technology) has become outdated and therefore useless. While the knowledge with which our children graduate from school still has an estimated half life of 20 years, this time is just one year for the field of computer technology. Or in other words, after one year, 50 % of the knowledge that is needed to be in command of computer technology will become outdated (see Figure 2).

The phenomenon of accelerated change in technology has enormous implications for curriculum development. The procedure of defining necessary skills on the basis of an analysis of the actual work situation and then creating a training curriculum on the basis of this documented analysis is no longer feasible. A substantial part of the curriculum would already be outdated once it is implemented.

Figure 2: The Accelerated Pace of Technological Change

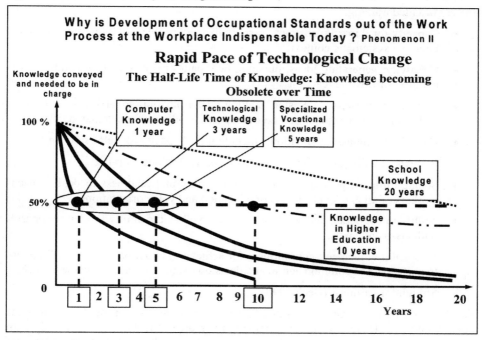

Source: IBM Data, n.d.

We are experiencing a dramatic shift of paradigms in training in which the actual situation at the workplace is undergoing continuous change. A sensitive, change-oriented and well-monitored approach to training has to be implemented in order to cope with these challenges.

The problem that we are facing in technical training today is an unawareness of the qualification requirements of the future, even in a year from now. The need for training in the absence of secured objectives requires a tremendous shift in paradigms. We owe it to the foresight of the "Club of Rome" that as early as 1978, new paradigms had already been outlined:

> "Since we do not know today what we need to know and master tomorrow, learning has to be anticipatory to enable us to adapt to new challenges in our work, and since the steadily growing complexity of work renders it impossible for an individual to be in charge of it all, learning has to be participatory to enable us to work in teams and networks" (Botkin, Mahdi, Mirzea 1978).

With "anticipation" and "participation" as the crucial orientation marks, training today has to be very different from the traditional "get prepared for the job and then 'perform' as long as you are on it" approach. "Formal" qualifications such as a willingness for lifelong learning, creativity, and capacity for assessing situations have gained enormous importance in the training of k-workers. Beck has compiled the following list of formal qualifications which have to be given high priority in an advanced concept of work-process oriented training:

- Capacity for thinking: abstract, logical, planned, problem-solving thinking, thinking in a systematic context,

- Creativity: generating ideas, pursuing new pathways in search of solutions, capability for flexible reactions,

- Capability to master decision making: determination to arrive at decisions, ability to make decisions, self consciousness, readiness for calculated risks,

- Capacity for assessing situations: including the capacity for self-criticism,

- Permanent willingness for continuous learning: lifelong learning,

- Social attitudes: personal responsibility, ability and readiness to deal with co-workers of all age levels, levels of education and value orientations,

- Ability to cooperate and work in teams as well as the ability to identify oneself with tasks and goals,

- Personal involvement: commitment for achieving, target orientation, willingness to participate in common action and decision making, reliability, perseverance,

- Straightforwardness (Beck 1998).

Yet, it would be misleading to assume that just mastering these formal qualifications alone would be sufficient to stay in command in an area of technology. It is only with the additional assistance of content-based in-depth knowledge and skills in a particular area that an individual can be equipped to venture into the new technological challenges ahead (Gerstenmaier 1999). The focus of content-based expertise must be on the work process.

It will be the skilful integration of selected formal qualifications and content-based in-depth knowledge and skills in a particular area of technology which will secure successful, development-oriented performance at the workplace (as demonstrated in Figure 3). For making this approach to training operational, the full potential of self-directed learning needs to be activated.

Making Training for K-Workers Operational: Worldwide Two Competing Approaches

In order to carry the training of k-workers into operationalization, we must refer back to the existing systems of training worldwide and their underlying approaches.

Figure 3: Visualizing the Concept of Training for the Actual Situation at the Workplace

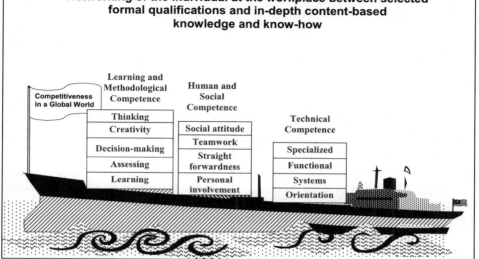

Source: Fadzliah Kamaruddin; Hofmann; DSP, updated 2005

There are endless national variations regarding how training is conducted, yet, two approaches worldwide have gained international reputation and are competing with each other. They are as follows:

- Competency-Based (Education and) Training (CBET) which is predominantly skills-assessment oriented,

- Experience-Based (Education and) Training (EBET), which is predominantly work-process oriented.

Very often competency-based training is seen as being in competition with the "dual" system of training, which is an irrelevant equation since it compares a training approach with a training system. It would instead be correct to refer to experience-based training as the approach underlying training in the "dual" system.

It is not the intention of this paper to provide an account of the historical roots of these approaches, nor to elaborate on a detailed comparison. It is our thesis that both approaches differ in their intended areas of activity. This becomes apparent when the respective areas of activity are located within their parameters of training. We have already discussed how competency-based training focuses on the assessment of skills for job competence. Experience-based training, on the other hand, addresses the in-structional process itself (cf. Gert Loose: Can We Link and Match Training in the "Dual System" with Competency-Based Training, in Chapter 2).

The complementary nature of both approaches seems to suggest that it may be desirable to combine them. Competency-based training focuses on the definition of skills for job competence without addressing the instructional process as such. On the other hand, experience-based training addresses the instructional process, yet, seems to have less regard for the "ceiling" on the acquisition of skills. That is, the sequence of targeted skills which, once mastered, render an individual competent for performance in a job.

The guidance that could potentially come from competency-based training in defining the objectives of training programmes cannot become effective at present for two reasons. Firstly, the "longevity" of the defined skills for job competence in high-tech occupations is no longer sufficient to provide direction for training. And secondly, a closer look at the sequence of targeted skills defined with the instruments of competency-based training reveals that they are "functional" (i.e. directly operational) in nature. The most important "extra-functional" skills which address behavioural aspects at the workplace (such as punctuality and getting along with fellow workers in a team) cannot sufficiently be assessed with these instruments.

Experience-based training in essence relies on the training potential of actual work situations. This core aspect has become indispensable today because steadily increasing complexity and excessive pace of change in technology can only be grasped where it becomes effective at the workplace itself. Accordingly, training must be aligned with the actual situation at the workplace to utilize its full potential as a learning environment.

Experience-Based Training for Tomorrow's Qualification Needs

The importance of the workplace for the training of k-workers has already widely been accepted. The two following quotations, one from the international perspective and one from a national context, are just examples of the increasing recognition worldwide that training should heavily rely on the workplace as a learning environment.

> "... business and the labour market demand abilities and knowledge which are mainly acquired in work situations." Ulrich Hillenkamp, UNEVOC, 1999, p.50.

> "Only through an extensive cooperation between learning environments including the workplace, the quality of training can be improved." Rolf Weinstedt, Presentation KMK, 1997.

Ultimately the intentions of training must be geared towards performance in the actual work situation. Any attempts to completely replicate or simulate its parameters will be in vain. It is therefore deplorable that a comprehensive taxonomy of learning environments is still lacking. Such a taxonomy would elaborate on the learning potential which is inherent in the different learning environments and facilitate the identification of correlations between "types of learning" (such as learning abstract information, understanding natural science phenomena through self-conducted experiments etc.) and "particular learning environments".

The supreme role of the workplace as a learning environment becomes apparent just from a provisional appraisal of "matching" types of learning and learning environments.

Yet, considering the complex tasks of k-workers, it is also obvious that we need the classroom (and other varieties of institutional settings) as an additional learning environment for effective training. This insight is the conceptual cornerstone of any "dual" system of training (see Figure 4).

Figure 4: The Need to Combine Different Learning Environments

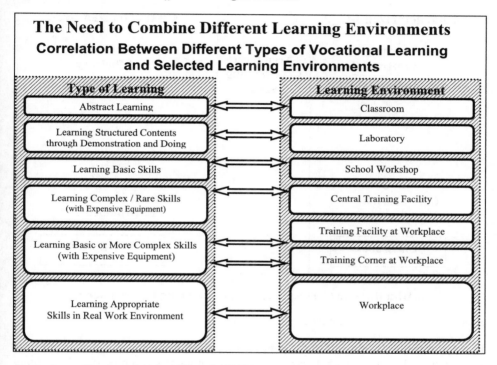

Source: Loose; Forschungsbericht, 1988, revised 2004

Consequently the training of k-workers requires the combination of two different domains: the "training institution" and the "enterprise" and possibly their variations such as the laboratory on the institutional side and the training corner at the workplace on the enterprise side. Often this is referred to as "theory" being addressed in an institutional setting, while "practice" is attended to at the workplace.

Attributing the role of the supreme learning environment for training to the workplace requires the acknowledgement of enterprises (or in other words of the private sector) as the main stakeholder in training. Consequently, when designing the most effective learning constellation for the training of k-workers, we must do much more than "patch" learning environments together. There are stakeholders, each with different mindsets, behind these learning environments and their successful cooperation has to be secured.

Figure 5: The Two Domains Constitute the "Dual System of Training"

The Two Domains Which Constitute the „Dual System of Training"		
Training Institution		**Enterprise**
Characterized by:		**Characterized by:**
• Learning • Protected Zone • Individual Care	**Need for a Coordinating Agent**	• Production • Efficiency • Profitability
⬇ **Core Learning Environment:** Classroom		⬇ **Core Learning Environment:** Workplace
... with the Two Corresponding Core Learning Environments		

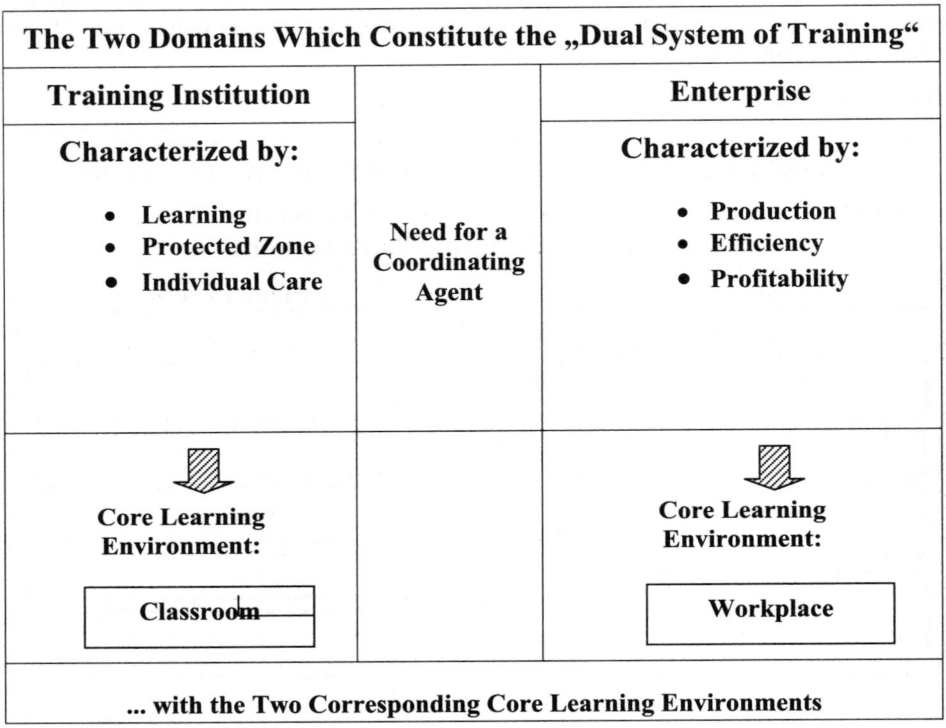

Source: Loose;Dual System Project, 2005

In order to render training effective, pathways for solid, harmonious, flexible, and most of all powerful cooperation between the main stakeholders in training (i.e. the training institutions and the private sector) have to be established. It should be in the interest of every single enterprise in the private sector that the process of forming partnerships with training institutions is initiated with all determination (cf. Blings 2007).

The secret of success for dual system training following the experience-based approach lies in mobilizing the training potential of the private sector and in identifying and operating smart mechanisms of interlinking "institutional" and "enterprise-based" learning and training activities. Again, the permanent challenge for the establishment of successful dual-system training arrangements lies in the difference in mindset between the respective stakeholders behind the two domains of learning and training (see Figure 5).

The Private Sector as Lead Agent for Dual-System Training: Alternative Scenarios for Further Development

We are confident that private sector enterprises are aware of the precious capacity which lies in Malaysia's workforce. We are also confident that they will use the opportunity to open their doors for creating the necessary training infrastructure, forming the basis for unfolding the full potential of workforce productivity that the nation can deliver. This chapter will not make any detailed suggestions for the actual design of the training infrastructure. However, it is important to note that any form of training has to incorporate the actual workplace in order to be effective. The enhancement of dual system arrangements in training must be considered a top priority for improving the effectiveness of training. These arrangements span the whole scope of potential cooperation, ranging from 0 % (i.e. "separation", in the sense of non-communication and unawareness of each other's actual training needs and provision) to 100 % (i.e. "integration", in the sense of completely integrating learning events directly into the work process). Their compilation in one scheme provides the platform for creating the operational structure of a "Dual Technical Education and Vocational Training Culture" (see Figure 6).

Figure 6: The Dual Training Culture - Selected Tools for the Integration of Learning and Working

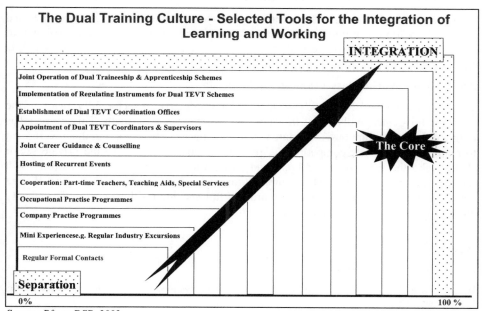

Source: Pforte;DSP, 2002

In its immediate application, the scheme of a Dual TEVT Culture can assist training institutions and enterprises alike in determining their present position regarding dual system training, and to establish development plans for enhancing the dual orientation of their training efforts. Strategically this scheme can serve as a reference map for designing the operational structure of work-oriented training for Malaysia. The creative interaction between stakeholders involved in training within the Malaysian society and culture will determine how this operational structure should take its shape. Potentially this may result in either one of four possible scenarios of development:

- Scenario 1: The private sector does not enhance its involvement in dual-system oriented training. This results in no significant change in the present system of training.

- Scenario 2: The private sector prefers a mainly unregulated enhancement of dual-system structures. This would mean that from enterprise to enterprise, and from training institution to training institution, individual measures for enhancing dual structures would be applied.

- Scenario 3: The private sector voices a strong commitment regarding the dual orientation of training. Subsystems of public training providers become partially involved in dual-system training with the private sector. In addition, companies and training institutions enhance their dual orientation on an individual basis.

- Scenario 4: The private sector voices a strong commitment regarding the dual orientation of training and calls for a nationwide regulated system involving all public training providers. A national dual training system involving all public subsystems of training is implemented.

An Outlook: World Class Training for Malaysia

The main purpose of this book is to make Malaysia's private sector fully aware of the need for full-scale involvement in training as a strategy for growth. This chapter has outlined the conceptual basis for mutual action by the private sector and the government to maintain Malaysia's competitive edge in the global market. Yet, the private sector should take the lead. It is our hope and expectation that business and industry will initiate, and bring to full thrust, a campaign for dual system training in Malaysia. We are certain that the government is ready to provide full backing for this boost in the capacity and quality of training for the country.

References

Beck, U. (1998). *a+l/Wirtschaft,* No. 10.

Blings, J. (2007): *Informelles Lernen in der Kreislauf- und Abfallwirtschaft - Eine empirische Studie.* Bertelsmann. Bonn

Botkin, J.W.; Mahdi, E.; Mirzea, M. (1978). *No Limits to Learning.* Oxford.

Bruner, J. (1972). *The Relevance of Education.* . Allen and Unwin. London

Department of Statistics, Malaysia (2001). *Monthly Manufacturing Statistics Malaysia.* www.statistics.gov.my

Fortune (2006). *The World's Largest Corporations.* 16.02.2006. www.fortune.com

Gerstenmaier, J. (1999). *Denken benötigt Wissen.* GdWz Vol. 10, No. 2, p. 65-67.

Kerka, S. (n.y.). *Competency-Based Education and Training: Myths and Realities.* ERIC Clearinghouse for Adult Ed. Columbus, Ohio.

Markowitsch, I. et al. (2002): *Competence and Human Resource Development in Multinational Companies. A comparative analysis between Austria, the Netherlands, and the United Kingdom.* Cedefop: Thessaloniki.

National Council for Vocational Qualifications (1995). *NVQ criteria and guidance.* Employment Department. London.

Ninth Malaysia Plan 2006-2010 (2006). *Ninth Malaysia Plan 2006-2010.* EPU, Prime Minister's Department. Kuala Lumpur.

Norton, R.E. (1997). *DACUM Handbook. 2nd Edition.* CTE: Ohio State University. Columbus Ohio.

Sarji, A. (ed.) (1997). *Malaysia's Vision 2020.* Petaling Jaye, Pelanduk.

Second Industrial Master Plan 1996-2005 (1996). *Second Industrial Master Plan 1996-2005.* Ministry of International Trade and Industry. Kuala Lumpur.

The Third Outline Perspective Plan 2001-2020 (2001). *The Third Outline Perspective Plan 2001-2020.* EPU, Prime Minister's Department. Kuala Lumpur.

UNESCO's Programme for the First Decade of the New Millenium" (1999). *UNESCO's Second International Congress on Technical and Vocational Education.* Seoul, Republic of Korea, April 29, 1999.

World Bank (2006). *World Development Indicators Database. February 2006.* www.worldbank.org

World Trade Organisation (2004). www.wto.org/english/res_e/statis_e/its2005_e/its05_overview e.pdf, 20.02.2006.

Work Process Analyses – An Essential Tool for Qualification and Curriculum Research

Georg Spöttl; Matthias Becker

Objectives of the Work Process-Analysis

The Importance of a Methodological Orientation of Qualification Research as a Basis for Curriculum Construction

The discussion on learning field orientation, learning in and within occupational work processes and a *work-oriented turning point* (cf. Fischer 2003, Rauner 2004, p. 9) raises the question of what should be the sources for structuring and shaping curricula[1]. Various aspects of the world of work are being investigated by qualification research as possible sources . The content to be included in the vocational curriculum is crucially determined by the orientation chosen for qualification research. Hence applied research methods represent the key to the quality of training. They determine what is to be assessed in the work process and thus considered for inclusion in the curriculum, and what can be considered at all.

Curricula reflect prior decisions about what contents should be learned and what are appropriate teaching and learning processes. The central issues for qualification research which aims to support curriculum development are therefore: Can the central, path breaking work coherences be elucidated by these methods?[2] Based on the research results – and in the light of a later transfer to instruction – can teaching and learning arrangements be developed which allow for the qualification of employees in occupational fields of actions? Do the identified contents represent a true picture of a qualificational profile or an occupation? What is their importance for developing competencies for future professional life and personality development?

These questions are of course relevant for the analysis of the occupational world of work. Qualification research in Germany is considered a revived dimension which must be newly established after a wave of scientification and humanistic orientation in education (Georg et al., 2004). In contrast to the German discussion of vocational education (cf. Lisop 2003, p. 301; Pahl 2005, p. 79; Rauner 2004) *work orientation* is the core of curriculum construction in many countries. Procedures[3] used for curriculum construction, such as task inventories, job and task analysis, analysis of occupational functions or the DACUM procedure, widespread in work sciences, all focus on the *work*

---

1   So far the discussion on learning fields often raises the suspicion that it is directed backwards and that it is approaching the behaviouristic discussion of learning fields.
2   We would like to stress that we do not intend to discuss exemplary contents but path breaking work coherences.
3   Procedures represent the research methodological framework for the use of one or several methods. They predetermine the structures and the mode of operation for the use of methods.

(cf. Fretwell; Lewis, Deij 2001; Schryvers; Van Gyes; Vandenbrande 2004). The work orientation as such is, however, not sufficient to assure the quality of a curriculum. A curriculum must do more than assure success in the labour market and utilization of the qualifications. It must also adapt to changes in the world of work and take into account the multi-dimensional requirements for employees/apprentices and the learning process. These are all normative prerequisites for the "quality" of a curriculum which are subject to different criteria according to the purpose of the curriculum. For example: The learning process does not play any role in the curricula of the United Kingdom it is learning outcomes and their assessability that count. This was underpinned by a recent reform project in the United Kingdom to develop new frameworks and descriptors for a learning outcome-based level classification (cf. QCA, 2004; http://www.qca.org.uk). Within the Dual System, a curriculum for initial vocational training must yield different achievements than a curriculum for in-firm further training. It might therefore be reasonable to use different methods to support the development of different curricula. As for vocational education, however, we assume the following basic and generalized quality criteria for a vocational curriculum:

- The curriculum defines the content which presently and in the future will be necessary to cope with tasks in the occupation (international: the fields of activity). *Content* thus always means the *work* content rather than the *specialized* content derived from scientific systematics (cf. Rauner 2004, p. 9ff.). Thus the subject is the occupational subject rather than the specialized science of a technology.

- The competency requirements specified in a curriculum are oriented towards the content.

- The structure and composition of a curriculum underpin the conceptualisation of teaching and learning arrangements for the educational goal to be reached.

- The curriculum is temporally stable. It needs not necessarily be revised to reflect changes in work, technology and education, but refers to temporally stable categories.

We base our assumptions on the reference definition established by Frey and the consequent functions of a curriculum. However, we put "the teaching and learning arrangement" in place of "instruction" in order to keep the issue of the learning environment open: *"The curriculum is the systematic image of the intended instruction during a certain period of time as a consistent system with several areas for an optimal preparation, implementation and evaluation of instruction" (Frey 1971, p. 50).*

Procedures and instruments respectively and the methods applied within this framework are directly related to the quality of the curriculum thus described. Weaknesses of the curriculum construction may be attributed to neglecting the work coherences when considering the above mentioned criteria. Identified conceptual weaknesses are, for example:

- "Link of occupational profiles to the surface of technological change or to a unilateral technology orientation;

- Occupations as a bundle of activities according to the performance principle (e.g. turning, milling) which are set up in an analysis-synthesis-process (performance analysis and synthetisation of work tasks);

- Correspondence of industrial and trade occupations with the specialized systematics of technological sciences rather than with the work task structures of the world of work;

- Discrepancy between the contents of occupational profiles and corporate work performances" (Spöttl 2000, p. 206).

With the help of vocational educational scientific work process analyses, such weaknesses of curriculum construction should be prevented by focussing qualification research on work coherences and the dimensioning of skilled work.

Objectives of Work Process Analyses with a Scientific Orientation

Work process analyses with a scientific orientation in vocational educational sciences comprise three objectives. They should help to:

(1) Identify the *competencies* for the coping and shaping of occupational work tasks;

(2) Access the most important coherences for *competency development*; and

(3) Determine the *work process knowledge* for the shaping of business and work processes.

With their three categories of objectives, i.e. *competency, competency development* and *work process knowledge*, these objectives hint at competing principles for determining the contents of curricula. Reetz and Seyd identified three different curriculum structures and approaches (science principle, personality principle and situation principle; cf. Reetz; Seyd 1983, 1995); well in advance of the introduction of learning fields they predicted that the principle of personality would become increasingly important in vocational educational practice (ibid, p. 204) and that the principle of science on the macro-level with its specialized scientific structures would continue to be dominant (ibid, p. 211). Work process-analyses take into consideration all three principles as conceived by vocational educational science:

- *Competences and the principle of science:* The systematic identification of competencies for coping with and shaping occupational work tasks can reflect these competencies in a systematic way. It is most important that regardless of the manifold problems of the practical realization (cf. Pahl 2005, p. 80) we assume that competencies can be assessed in a scientific and systematic way. It is to be noted that the science which is being discussed here does not count among the "classical" sciences (engineering science or educational sciences) but vocational sciences which – contrary to Pahl's opinion – have long ago left behind the status of inductive-pragmatic scientific approaches (ibid, p. 80). The purely specialised systematic structures of the engineering sciences or isolated pedagogical and hermeneutical structures of educational sciences are basically inadequate for defining competencies as they result in a curtailed understanding of them. The specialized systematic structures of the engineering sciences aim at knowledge or skills which are relevant for the engineer, but not for the skilled worker.

- The educational sciences are already dependent on interdisciplinary gateways in order to assess the object of vocational education[4]. The CEDEFOP definition, *"Competency is the ability to make use of knowledge, know-how and skills in a familiar and new coherence"* (Tissot 2004, S. 48) already emphasises the crucial importance of context (coherence) and application. However, the CEDEFOP definition implicitly assumes that competencies can be explicitly defined before being applied, and can thus be initially independent of real occupational action. This basic assumption – better known as intellectualistic legend – is, however, hardly tenable (cf. Ryle 1949; Neuweg 1999). To concentrate exclusively on "explicit knowledge" is not enough for vocational education which must always encompass "implicit knowledge", i.e. the knowledge developed *during* application and via experience. Implicit knowledge cannot be objectified, and in this context a competency is essentially a disposition for expert-like acting, the *skills*. Skills, however, are not derived from competency, but are themselves the image of competency. The implication for research methods is that skills themselves have to be surveyed and decoded. Or, as Rauner puts it referring to Bergmann (1995): *"The vocational educational research is all about ... the decoding of knowledge and skills incorporated in occupational work, organised in specialized domains"* (Rauner 2004, p. 33).

- *Competency development and the principle of personality*: It is a central assumption that competencies develop in the course of dealing with occupational work tasks and problems. This assumption is based on an extended definition of learning (cf. Becker; Spöttl; Stolte 2001) which includes the development of competencies. An analytical differentiation between specialized, personal and social competencies is not intended; instead they are regarded as the dimensions of occupational acting competency. Within the framework of work process analyses, *challenging situations, tasks and problems* are investigated – above all how they can be mastered. This survey yields results and findings on how the (occupational) development of the personality (by confrontation with them) can be best supported. Certain acting situations prove beneficial for competency development and in turn require the mastering of others. Work process analyses contribute to the accessibility of coherences and conditions "which allow for a support of the transition of one development level to another" (Rauner 1999, p. 431). The development is then "logical" in terms of continuous occupational competency. The adequate consideration of development tasks leads to a curriculum structured in a development logical way.

- *Work process knowledge and the situation principle*: Work process knowledge creates immediate coherence between the knowledge of corporate work organisation and specialized theoretical knowledge. Transfer activities are not required. It is the acting relevant knowledge of this coherence. It is closely

---

4   cf. Debates on the positioning of specialized didactics (Pahl/Schütter 2000; Herkner/Vermehr 2004).

linked to one's own work experience and knowledge of the corporate world. It *"means to understand the entire work process which involves the respective person complete with its product related, technical, work organisational, social and system oriented dimensions"* (Kruse 1986, p. 189). Exactly these dimensions can be determined by work process analyses and thus the acting conditions determined by organisational decisions and technological influences.

The following chapters will concentrate on examples of the application of work process analyses to construct curricula for two occupational profiles (tool maker, automotive mechatronic) which have been developed for the Dual Training System in Malaysia (Sistem Latihan Dual Nasional) introduced in January 2005. Prior to this, the embedding of work process analyses into a vocational scientifically oriented set of research instruments and the basic methodological concept of work process analyses will be outlined.

With a critical reflection of different procedures of qualification research at the conclusion of this essay we will summarize and highlight why work process analyses are an indispensable element of qualification research.

Work Process Analyses in Vocational Education Research

Work process analyses are always carried out in connection with other instruments of vocational educational research and never stand alone. They serve to access the occupational skilled work *from inside* and need to be embedded into a more comprehensive research concept (cf. Becker 2004, p. 169ff.). Four different research levels can be identified, each focussing on a different kind of analysis (cf. Table 1).

As a rule these levels are traversed during the research process in the listed order. Sufficient findings on the individual levels must, however, be available in order to be able to resort to existing material. This is especially true on the level of the occupational and sector specific structures which are normally well developed and which make the use of (additional) sector analyses (cf. Spöttl 2005) obsolete. The latter, however, does not mean in any case that the already existing findings should not be taken into consideration.

These research levels reveal a close affinity to the "levels of occupational profiles" (cf. Lisop 2003, p. 317) which are used as an empirical foundation for curriculum content by Huisinga and Lisop (cf. Huisinga; Lisop 2002). Actually more comprehensive analysis and reflection levels are applied whenever a drifting apart of qualification and curriculum research is identified.

Table 1: Levels of Vocational Education Research

Level	Instrument	Methods
Occupational and sector structures as well as comprehensive impact on all occupations	Sector analyses	Vocational educational analyses of documents (sector reports, occupational statistics, literature, technological developments), quantitative surveys on the domain and on qualification practice
Organisational structures of occupational work processes	Case studies	Task inventories, order analyses, company visits, analysis of corporate processes and key data
Competencies in business and work processes	Work process analyses	Observation of work, acting oriented specialized interviews and expert talks
Importance of identified competencies and work tasks for the occupation	Expert skilled worker workshops	Brainstorming, meta-plan techniques and specialised discussions for a participative evaluation of the identified work tasks. Evaluation and weighting of the tasks for the development oriented arrangement in vocational educational plans

Two methods are predominantly used within the framework of work process analyses: the *observation of work* (cf. Becker 2005b) and the *expert interview* or the *acting oriented specialized interview* respectively (cf. Becker 2005a). The observation of work aims at decoding those situative work practices which lead to successful occupational acting. This technique – closely linked to recent trends of the *studies of work* – allows for delving deeply into the practice community of skilled work. It is not distant observation using pre-determined observation criteria, but the closest possible observation of occupational practice. The acting oriented specialised interview is also closely linked with work observation. The researcher tries to clarify open questions and discusses and opens up intentions and applied knowledge. If successful, this approach allows a high degree of objectification of implicit knowledge by trying to understand all moments within the acting context (*context oriented* objectification, cf. Becker 2003, p. 65).

The Implementation of Work Process Analyses – the Example of Malaysia

Weaknesses of the Competency Based Approach

The implementation of work process analyses will be illustrated by describing the curriculum development process for two occupational profiles in the "newly industrialised" country Malaysia (cf. Figure 2). These were developed for the newly introduced national dual training system (cf. http://www.dualsystemproject.net), which is to replace and modernise the "Competency-based" system with its DACUM based job profiles and occupational standards (National Occupational Skill Standards – NOSS), introduced in 1993. The NOSS directory currently includes 581 NOSS profiles with their respective Curricula (cf. http://www.nvtc.gov.my/NOSS/index_prog1.php).

Figure 1: *Competency Based Approach for the Development of "National Occupational Skills Standards (NOSS)*

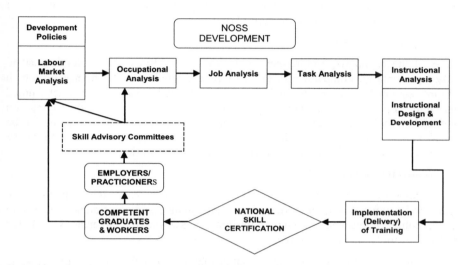

Source: http://www.trainingmalaysia.com/mlvk/ NOSS (English).shtml

Industry in Malaysia is developing rapidly, and requires comprehensively trained skilled workers[5]. Competency-Based-Training (CBT) according to the British model, which is mainly oriented towards an adaptive qualification and functions, seems to be less and less adequate for this aim.

NOSS curricula describe very narrow fields of tasks (Duties) and highly fragmented tasks (Tasks) which can no longer cope with the ranges of tasks facing skilled workers in modern production and service concepts. Spöttl states:

> "The high risk linked to this approach is that the instruction process is split in a similar way resulting in a 'Tayloristic' method of teaching which reflects the Tayloristic division of labour of the 'old production concepts' in factories" (Spöttl 2002, S. 20).

This is partly due to the concentration during the design of instruction (cf. Figure 1) on "learning outcomes" which can be most easily realised by precisely defined and closely delimited work and learning steps. On the other hand, teachers and trainers involved in instructional design lack information on the work processes and work coherences which were not assessed through the procedures of "job" and "task analysis" and therefore could not be taken into consideration for designing the curricula. In addition a syste-

---

5   In Malaysia they are called knowledge workers (k-workers).

matic teacher training is necessary to enable teaching staff to translate work process oriented curricula into didactic concepts.

Conducting Work Process Analyses

Curricula which are prepared using work process analyses rely on the definition of core work processes, work process oriented core work tasks and the relevant competencies which have to be identified through visits to representative companies. The process of curriculum development has three phases (cf. Figure 2) and involves a group of curriculum developers, rather than an individual.

1   Preparation Phase

Analysis of the economic, employment and training structures of a sector is used to identify representative companies for the work process analyses. The enterprises which stand for "best practice" in the particular sector are selected. Best practice is determined taking into consideration certain key data on the one hand and relying on recommendations by sector experts on the other. The number of the companies to be surveyed varies – based on experience so far – between 4 and 20 according to the structure of the sector and the variety and complexity of the work processes.

2   Realisation Phase

In case studies of at least one day's duration, work processes in the companies are surveyed and key persons are interviewed. A semi-standardized questionnaire is used to ensure that observations and interviews contribute to assessing the dimensions of skilled work (objects, tools, methods and requirements for skilled work).

A special advantage of work processes is that problems and challenges can immediately be linked to the object of skilled work (cf. Figure 3). It is thus clear which competencies are *really* applied and necessary to cope with the work processes. There are often considerable differences between the planning of work in anticipation and its actual execution (cf. Drescher 1996, p. 28) – and indeed, much of the execution of work cannot be systematically planned in advance, but requires improvisation and a feeling for adequate approaches (cf. Gerds 2001; Bauer et al., 2002). These details can only be assessed with the help of work process analyses. Not all of them can of course be reflected in the curriculum ultimately produced. The curriculum developer, however, gets a deeper insight into the work coherences. The isolation of individual tasks can thus be prevented because the curriculum developer has developed a notion for the work process knowledge via the research process and can thus handle the description of educational contents in a more sensitive way (cf. Spöttl 2003).

Figure 2: Survey and Development Phases of Curriculum Development

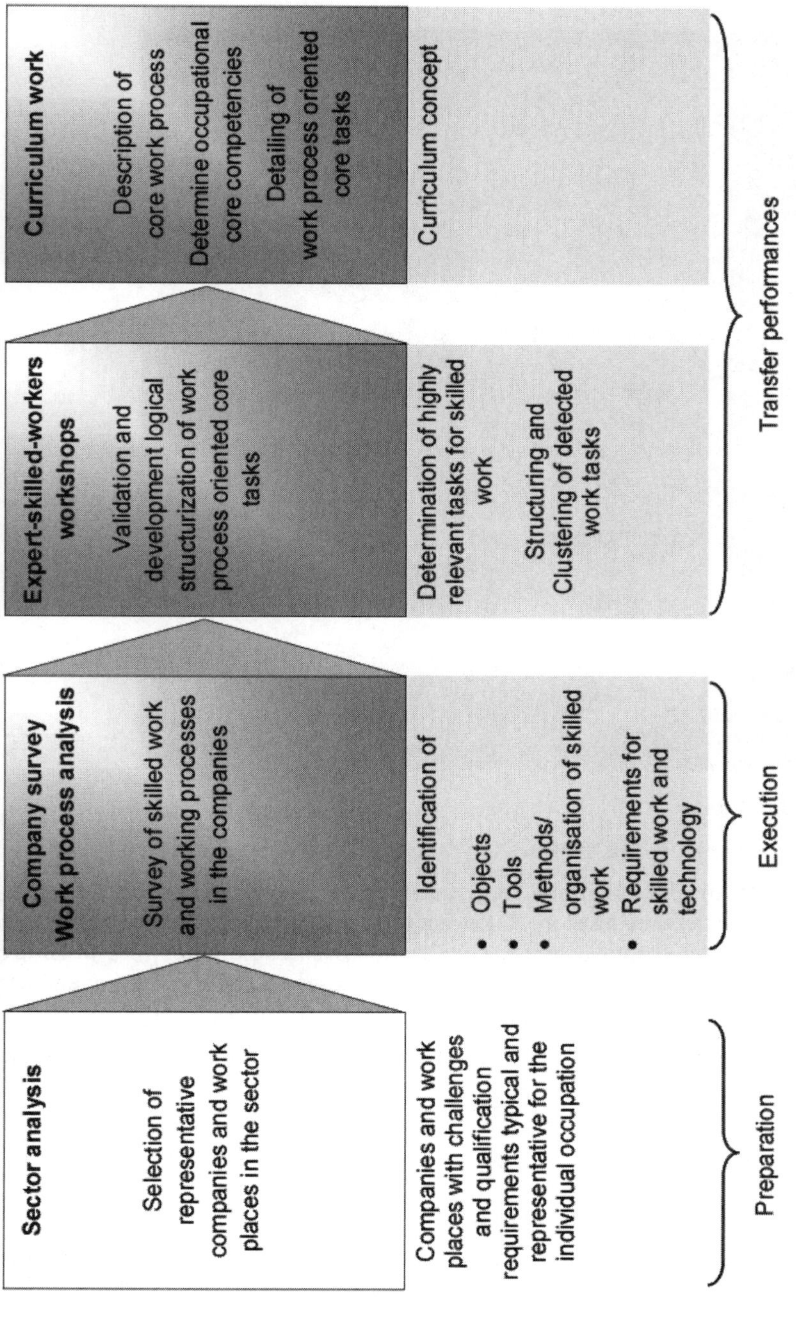

Figure 3:   *Glimpse at a Work Process Analysis Regarding the Repair of a Mould for a Die by a Tool Maker*

3   Transfer Phase

Subsequent to the work process analyses the following aims are realized step by step:

- The results are discussed and (pre)structured in a workshop involving all researchers/ curriculum developers. During this workshop, the identified variety of tasks are clustered into coherent core work tasks. These core work tasks are always oriented towards the central work processes of skilled workers and are therefore named core work processes;

- First concepts for the core curricula[6] are developed with the aid of a draft for the curriculum structure;

---

6   In Malaysia these are called "National Occupational Core Curricula – NOCC". The curricular description of a core work task is considered a NOCC and the sum of all NOCCs forms the core occupational profile/ National Occupational Curriculum.

- In an expert skilled worker workshop, acknowledged experts in the particular skill review and validate the first drafts of the work task designs and contents descriptions;

- The core curriculum is revised and the final product of the curriculum is set up complete with a description of the occupational profile.

From DACUM Facilitator to Work Process Facilitator – Experiences with Work Process Analyses

The National Occupational Curriculum (NOC) for the two occupational profiles "Toolmaker" and "Automotive Mechatronic" was developed within 14 days by the authors in cooperation with around 20 curriculum developers of the MLVK (National Vocational Training Council), following the procedure described above. This time included introducing the curriculum developers to the philosophy and approaches of the work process oriented procedure.

The majority of the curriculum developers are experienced "DACUM facilitators" and familiar with the development of curricula with precise descriptions of "duties" and "tasks" as well as the relevant lists of contents. The DACUM approach calls for facilitated workshops of experts of the occupation to be analysed, who should be familiar with the entire range of tasks of the occupation. The approach applies a very rigorous framework of definitions and activities well known to the curriculum developers and easy to apply away from the reality of the workplace. When confronted with work process analyses they first had to realise that the content coherences within the work processes are so comprehensive that they cannot simply be broken down analytically. In addition they faced a highly complex specialized vocabulary which was partly specific to the relevant company, corporate culture and practice community.

Thus the DACUM facilitators had no problems compiling pages and pages of listings of the individual tasks of the work processes, identifying the required tools and determining the necessary knowledge and skills. The greatest difficulties came with preparing detailed work task descriptions, and identifying the specialized occupational problems and their requirements for the work tasks.

The DACUM experts often interpreted "work process" as the process of developing a *product*. The same problematic understanding was partly true for the term "work order orientation". Such misunderstandings often resulted in focusing not on the competency of the skilled worker, but the competency for shaping products, orders or business processes and thus the value-added aspect of the work process. Consequently the curricula often split up the competencies concentrating on "*part products*" (aggregates, order parts) instead of on the process coherences inherent in skilled work. This results in typical DACUM task lists, for example for the "Motor Vehicle Mechanic". According to the old NOSS Curricula these lists are structured according to vehicle components:

The corresponding duties are as follows:

- Service carburation system,
- Service diesel fuel system,

- Service vehicle electrical system,
- Perform engine repair by carrying out engine overhaul,
- Service electronic fuel injection system,
- Repair clutch system,
- Repair manual drive train,
- Repair brake system,
- Repair steering system,
- Service turbocharger.

The tasks of each of these fields are individual and partly incoherently listed performances, for example for the field of tasks "Repairs clutch system":

- Check condition of clutch system,
- Replace clutch cable,
- Bleed clutch hydraulic system,
- Overhaul clutch master pump/ slave cylinder,
- Replace clutch pressure plate, disc and bearing.

For the tool maker, who is more closely involved in industrial production processes, rather than assessing the central work tasks for a skilled worker, the work processes were originally split into individual processes along with the production process of mould-and-die tools. The formulation of coherent work processes for tool makers called for an extensive discussion highlighting the importance of the different approaches. Figure 4 shows the first draft of core work processes which was realized the day after the work process analyses.

It was especially difficult to determine the vertical and horizontal boundaries for the "Toolmaker core occupational profile". The work process analyses revealed that the toolmakers have to possess a sound overview knowledge of the entire production process of mould-and-die tools as well as jig and fixtures. They do not, however, design moulds or generate 3D construction data (cf. Figure 4, mould design) nor do they produce zero series (Mould Trial, T0). The first task is confined to engineers, the latter to machine setters. The toolmaker has to cooperate closely with both of them in order to remedy construction faults and to identify and repair faults identified in zero series.

The NOSS System in Malaysia works with a qualification framework of five levels (cf. Figure 5), http://www.trainingmalaysia.com/mlvk/NOSS(english).shtml) and assigns occupational profiles for skilled workers to levels 1 to 3 (cf. Table 2).

Table 2: *Vertical Delimitation of Occupational Profiles in the NOSS-System*

Level 5	Manufacturing Engineer CAD/CAM (Jurutera Pembuatan CAD/CAM)
Level 4	Plastic Moulding Designer (Pereka Acuan Plastik)
Level 3	Senior Toolmaker – Plastic Injection Mould (Pembuat Perkakasan Kanan – Acuan Suntikan Plastik)
Level 2	Toolmaker Plastic Injection Mould (Pembuat Perkakasan Acuan Suntikan Plastik)
Level 1	Various profiles on the level of elementary metal working (Milling Operation Machinist, Turning Operation Machinist, Grinding Operation Machinist, General Machinist) up to machine operators (Plastic Production "Injection Moulding")

Figure 4: Product Development Process (left, vertical) and Transversal and Comprehensive Core Work Processes of Toolmakers as a First Draft for the „Toolmaker Curriculum".

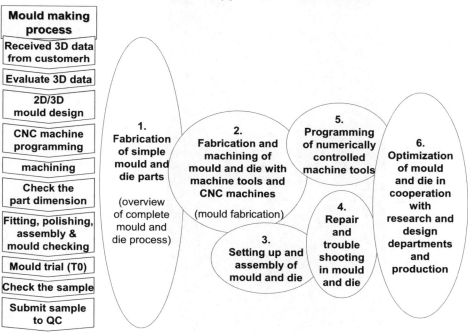

The profiles are also very closely delimited horizontally. Thus there is a toolmaker for plastic injection mould (cf. Table 2), for press tools and for jigs and fixtures etc.

Due to their experience with work process analyses, the Malaysian curriculum developers came increasingly to understand the need for broadly designed occupational profiles which safeguard a flexible use and expandable competency profiles along with increasing work requirements. The training of a "toolmaker" without a specialization for a certain technology (plastic, metal) or a single procedure (injection mould, pressing, stamping) – at first completely beyond the imagination of the curriculum developers – became more realistic along with the increasing findings from the work process analyses.

Figure 5:   *Qualification Framework of the Malaysian Training System*

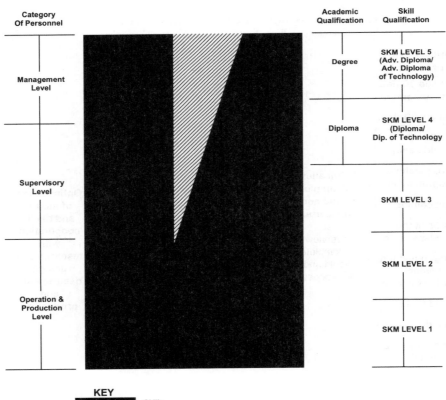

This necessity became equally important during the work process analyses for the "Automotive Mechatronic". The companies surveyed complained about the poor level of the national profiles, and ambitious companies increasingly implemented company and sector specific qualification programmes to compensate for the shortcomings of the dissected NOSS profiles (e.g. ProTAP-programme for the automotive sector, cf. http://www.otomotif.com.my/).

During the transfer phase and after identifying the core work tasks and the occupational profile, first drafts for the curricula were set up as follows:

(1) Description of the *core work task* (CORE WORK PROCESS),

(2) Determination of *the competencies to be developed* for the described core task (OCCUPATIONAL CORE COMPETENCIES) and

(3) Documentation of the *objects* of the core work task and the respective required *tools, methods, the organisation* as well as the multi-dimensional *requirements* (DETAILING THE CORE WORK PROCESS).

As for the formulation of contents for the curriculum, DACUM facilitators referred to formulation ordinances and looked for similar ones for the description of work process oriented curricula. The following explanations were provided for support:

Core work task: The description is done by coherently documenting the basic work process (of the skilled workers, cf. above) by answering the following questions:

– What must the skilled worker do in detail while coping with this task?

– What are the requirements for this task? How are they coped with?

– Which problems have to be solved?

Competencies: The competencies for the task are described by a verb referring to the object of work and by the denomination of the context with connection to the work process.

Objects: We are speaking of objects of skilled work (the customer, the faulty product or tool, ...) which are described in the form of work to be addressed or references made (relevant work steps, products, technology, phenomena).

Tools, methods, organisation: Identification of what is necessary and relevant for the performance of a work task.

Requirements: Requirements by the customers, the company (quality requirements, work safety), by the state and its legislation and regulations, by technology (standards and technical requirements) and by the skilled worker himself (working conditions).

After some practice and with the help of their experience acquired during the work process analyses and the design of the curricula, the participating curriculum developers are on the right path towards becoming *work process facilitators*.

Development of National Core Occupational Profiles – Results

After completion of the transfer phase (cf. above) the National Occupational Curricula with eight core work tasks each were available for both the *Automotive Mechatronic* and the *Toolmaker*. An example for a completely formulated NOCC is given in the following figure of core work task No. 7 of the Automotive Mechatronic "Diagnosis and repair of aggregates, component groups and elements".

The curricula are always taking into consideration national characteristics. One example is NOCC 8 for the automotive mechatronic. Compared to Europe, the Malaysian mechatronic in a workshop must master considerably higher repair depths in aggregates such as engines and gear boxes.

- Core occupational profile for the toolmaker:

- Design of mould and die,

- Fabrication and machining of mould and die,

- Assembling and disassembling of mould and die,

- Try out and trouble shooting of mould and die,

- Modification of mould and die as well as optimization,

- Maintenance, commissioning and repair of mould and die,

- Carrying through QC processes within fabrication and mould and die,

- Application of treatment processes relevant for mould and die.

Work Process Analyses – What Are Their Advantages
Compared to other Approaches?

In summary, by comparison with the work oriented procedures for curriculum development most established globally, work process analyses allow a deeper insight into the work processes and applied work process knowledge which in turn promotes access to vocational specialized coherences. The use of the findings from work process analyses for shaping curricula ensures the upholding of work coherences and the identification of holistic competencies. These competencies are directly linked to the work task and do not focus on performances or isolated actions but rather encompass all dimensions of occupational work.

Task inventories – widespread in work sciences – allow the developer to set up task examples from the world of work and even partly complete task lists which, however, may quickly become too complex and do not give any information on work coherences. They count among the procedures independent from persons (cf. Oesterreich/ Volpert 1987, p. 54ff.) and thus hardly give any indications for a core concern of curriculum development: the systematic support of vocational competency development.

Job analyses/ task analyses – and DACUM also belongs to this kind of methods – above all help to analyse tayloristically organised work to determine the training requirements for individual, well isolatable fields of actions: *Job Analysis* is a process to establish and document "the '*job relatedness*' of employment procedures such as training, selection, compensation, and performance appraisal" (http://www.job-analysis.net/).

Figure 6: Core Occupational Profile for the Automotive Mechatronic

	Core Occupational Profile for Automotive Mechatronic
	Range of Core Work Processes
Orientation and overview knowledge	**Work and learning area 1:** **The vehicle and basic service** 1. Standard service 2. Wear and tear repair
Coherent knowledge	**Work and learning area 2:** **The vehicle and its system function** 3. Trouble shooting, standardised diagnostic procedures and minor repair 4. General Inspection including emission testing
Detailed and functional knowledge	**Work and learning area 3:** **The vehicle and its component groups and modules** 5. Administrative Services and warranty 6. Standard Extensions and Accessory Installations
Specialised advanced knowledge	**Work and learning area 4:** **The car and its construction: Expert diagnosis and repair** 7. Diagnosis and repair of aggregates, component groups and elements 8. Repair of aggregates: Engine and gearbox

Figure 7a: NOCC 7: Diagnosis and Repair of Aggregates, Component Groups and Elements (PART 1 of 2)

NOCC 7:
DIAGNOSIS AND REPAIR OF AGGREGATES, COMPONENT GROUPS AND ELEMENTS
CORE WORK PROCESS

The repair of aggregates is carried through and causes for trouble in complex vehicle systems are repaired.

The task comprises repairs of aggregates, component groups and –elements, e.g. parts of the engine, differential, brake and steering system, chassis control and steering geometry for the reestablishment of functions and mode of operation.

Apart from methods of repair, focus is on the application, description, comparison and assessment of different aggregates and component-group oriented trouble shooting and diagnosis procedures especially in networked electronic vehicle systems.

OCCUPATIONAL CORE COMPETENCIES	Class-room	Work-shop
Determination of defects by analyzing the fault characteristic of components	X	X
Analyzing the effects of occurred component defects on the networked vehicle	X	X
Overhauling of engine components (cylinder head, …)		X
Maintenance/repairs of component assemblies and component elements using appropriate methods and procedures by applying relevant technical information systems, transparent documentation for customer, workshop and manufacturer	X	X
Repair and replacement of add-on aggregates, clutch and brake systems		X
Repair and adjustment of components in the steering system and chassis		X
Apply appropriate methods and procedures for checking, testing and tuning of restored component assembly and elements respectively and document it in a transparent way	X	X
Knowledge and confident application of different forms of communication with clients/customers and colleagues in relation to preparing, servicing and commissioning of vehicles	X	X

Figure 7b: NOCC 7: Diagnosis and Repair of Aggregates, Component Groups and Elements (PART 2 of 2)

DETAILING THE CORE WORK PROCESS

Objects of skilled work	Tools, methods used and organisation of skilled work	Requirements in terms of skilled work and technology in use
Repair of components to restore failure free functioning of the car: Fault characteristics and fault symptoms of components Ancillary components/engine components (replacement of cylinder head, oil pump, timing chain, ...) Add-on aggregates (starter, generator, turbo blower, ...) clutch and torque converter Drive shaft / propeller shaft (joint, bearing, shirt cuff) Steering gear, wheel suspension Brake cylinder and sub systems of safety and comfort systems (compressor, ABS, restraint system, ...) Mechatronic control systems of engine, drive system, steering, chassis, brake, safety systems, comfort systems	**Tools** Diagnosis databases Settings, tune-up specifications Computerized information systems and repair manuals Special assembly and disassembly tools measuring, test and diagnosis tools Clamping tools **Methods** Diagnosis procedures for component testing Visual, feel and acoustic checks Detection of damages Measuring and testing procedures for parts Replacement/repair methods for parts and components **Organisation** Organisation of efficient communication between customers and workshop Work organisation, team work Manage the work environment Providing, maintenance and ensuring of availability of special tools	**By customer:** Responsible order processing for a customer oriented repair Communication and dialogue to ensure the understanding of the customer explanations Carrying out of repair orders on schedule **By company:** Reliable decision making for optimal repair methods (replacement, repair, overhaul) **By skilled worker:** Choice of suitable special tools Regulations on company rules, stipulations, safety User friendly editing of data and information from the manufacturer Fast access to data and information for repair

"In the US, job analyses are widespread in order to set up 'job descriptions' (cf. *Dictionary of Occupational Titles* (DOT), http://www.occupationalinfo.org and http://www.onetcenter.org as well as O*NET Modell, Frieling 2004, p. 137ff.). The following definition of the term "job" proves that the definition of such "jobs" still do not have much in common with occupational thinking: "A *job* is a collection of tasks and responsibilities that an employee is responsible to conduct" (http://www.mapnp.org/library/staffing/specify/job_nlyz/job_nlyz.htm).

Finally the analysis of occupational functions (*functional analysis*) is worth mentioning. This is a deductive procedure and exclusively aims at the description of the "final condition" of an occupational action. Major functions and subsequently basic functions are determined with the help of *functional maps*. As soon as the functions are completely determined, the required competencies are defined. Functional analysis is often used for the development of competency based standards, e.g. for the NVQ in England and Wales. Work coherences do not play any role.

Wherever the world of work reaches a certain complexity and as soon as responsibility is transferred to the level of skilled work, work process analyses become essential in order to gain empirically confirmed findings for the required occupational competencies.

References

Becker, M. (2003): *Diagnosearbeit im Kfz-Handwerk als Mensch-Maschine-Problem.* W. Bertelsmann, Bielefeld.

Becker, M. (2004): *Zur Ermittlung von Diagnosekompetenz von Kfz-Mechatronikern – Ein berufswissenschaftliches Forschungskonzept.* In: Rauner, F. (Ed.): *Qualifikationsforschung und Curriculum.* W. Bertelsmann, Bielefeld: p. 167-184.

Becker, M. (2005a): *Handlungsorientierte Fachinterviews.* In: Rauner, F. (Ed.): *Handbuch Berufsbildungsforschung.* W. Bertelsmann Verlag, Bielefeld: p. 601-606.

Becker, M. (2005b): *Beobachtungsverfahren.* In: Rauner, F. (Ed.): *Handbuch Berufsbildungsforschung.* W. Bertelsmann Verlag, Bielefeld: p. 628-633.

Becker, M.; Spöttl, G.; Stolte, A. (2001): *ADAPT-Heritage. Neue Lernmodelle – Flexible und akzeptierte Wege zum Lernen für die Arbeitswelt.* NU-ADAPT, Bonn.

Bergmann, J. R. (1995): *"Studies of Work" – Ethnomethodologie.* In: Flick, U. et al. (Ed.): *Handbuch Qualitative Sozialforschung.* 2. Auflage. Beltz, Weinheim: p. 269-272.

Bauer, H. G.; Böhle, F.; Munz, C.; Pfeiffer, S.; Woicke, P. (2002): *Hightech-Gespür – Erfahrungsgeleitetes Arbeiten und Lernen in hoch technisierten Arbeitsbereichen.* Schriftenreihe des Bundesinstituts für Berufsbildung. Bertelsmann Verlag, Bielefeld.

Buch, M.; Frieling, E. (2004): *Die Reichweite von Tätigkeits- und Arbeitsanalysen für die Entwicklung beruflicher Curricula.* In: Rauner, F. (Ed.): *Qualifikationsforschung und Curriculum.* W. Bertelsmann, Bielefeld: p. 135-149.

Fischer, M. (2003): *Grundprobleme didaktischen Handelns und die arbeitsorientierte Wende in der Berufsbildung.* In: bwp@, Nr. 4. Online unter www.bwpat.de.

Fretwell, D. H.; Lewis, M. V.; Deij, A. (2001): *A Framework for Defining and Assessing Occupational and Training Standards in Developing Countries. Information Series No. 386.* World Bank, The Ohio State University, European Union, European Training Foundation.

Frey, K. (1971): *Theorien des Curriculums.* Beltz-Verlag, Weinheim und Basel.

Georg, W., Herkner, V.; Vermehr, B. (Ed.) (2004): *Berufsfeldwissenschaft – Berufsfelddidaktik – Lehrerbildung. Beiträge zur Didaktik gewerblich-technischer Berufsbildung.* Donat, Bremen.

Gerds, P. (2001): *Das Arbeitsprozesswissen erfahrener Facharbeiter beim Einschaben von ebenen Flächen höchster Qualität im Werkzeugmaschinenbau.* In: lernen & lehren, Heft Nr. 62, p. 53-59.

Huisinga, R.; Lisop, I. (2002): *Qualifikationsbedarf, Personalentwicklung und Bildungsplanung – Studien. Anstöße,* Band 14. GAFB Verlag, Frankfurt.

Lisop, I. (2003): *Paradigmatische Fundierung von Qualifikationsforschung und Curriculum-Konstruktion mittels "Arbeitsorientierte Exemplarik" (AOEX).* In: Huisinga, R.; Buchmann, U. (Ed.): *Curriculum und Qualifikation: Zur Reorganisation von Allgemeinbildung und Spezialbildung.* Anstöße, Band 15. GAFB Verlag, p. 295-328, Frankfurt.

Kruse, W. (1986): *Von der Notwendigkeit des Arbeitsprozess-Wissens.* In: Schweitzer, J. (Ed.): *Bildung für eine menschliche Zukunft.* Juventa, p. 188-193, Weinheim und München.

Neuweg, G. H. (1999): *Könnerschaft und implizites Wissen.* Münster et al.: Waxmann.

Oesterreich, R.; Volpert, W. (1987): *Handlungstheoretisch orientierte Arbeitsanalyse.* In: Kleinbeck, U.; Rutenfranz, J. (Hg.): *Arbeitspsychologie. Enzyklopädie der Psychologie,* Themenbereich D, Serie III, Band 1. et al.: Hogrefe, Göttingen: p. 43-73.

Pahl, J.-P. (2005): *Perspektiven der berufswissenschaftlichen und berufsdidaktischen Forschung. In: Zeitschrift für Berufs- und Wirtschaftspädagogik,* 101. Band, Heft 1. Franz Steiner Verlag, Stuttgart: p. 79-93.

Pahl, J.-P.; Schütte, F. (Ed.) (2000): *Berufliche Fachdidaktik im Wandel. Beiträge zur Standortbestimmung der Fachdidaktik Bautechnik.* Seelze-Velber: Kallmeyer.

QCA (2004): *Principles for a Credit Framework for England. Qualification and Curriculum Authority.* March 2004.

Rauner, F. (1999): *Entwicklungslogisch strukturierte berufliche Curricula: Vom Neuling zur reflektierten Meisterschaft.* In: *Zeitschrift für Berufs- und Wirtschaftspädagogik,* 95. Band, Heft 3. Steiner, Stuttgart: p. 424-446.

Rauner, F. (2004): *Qualifikationsforschung und Curriculum – ein aufzuklärender Zusammenhang.* In: Rauner, F. (Ed.): *Qualifikationsforschung und Curriculum.* W. Bertelsmann, Bielefeld: p. 9-43.

Reetz, L.; Seyd, W. (1983): *Curriculumtheorien im Bereich der Berufsbildung.* In: Hameyer, U., Frey, K., Haft, H. (Ed.): *Handbuch der Curriculumforschung.* Beltz, Weinheim, Basel: p. 171-192.

Reetz, L.; Seyd, W. (1995): *Curriculare Strukturen beruflicher Bildung.* In: Arnold, R.; Lipsmeier, A.: *Handbuch der Berufsbildung.* Leske+Budrich, Opladen: p. 203-219.

Ryle, G. (1949): *The Concept of Mind. London et al.: Hutchinson 1949* (verwendet in der deutschen Fassung: Der Begriff des Geistes. Reclam, Stuttgart: 2002).

Schryvers, E.; Van Gyes, G.; Vandenbrande, T. (2004): *Functional Map of a European Socio-Economic Research Project.* IES Report 414. The Institute for employment studies, Brighton

Spöttl, G. (2000): *Der Arbeitsprozess als Untersuchungsgegenstand berufswissenschaftlicher Qualifikationsforschung und die besondere Rolle von Experten(-Facharbeiter-)workshops.* In: Pahl, J.-P.; Rauner, F.; Spöttl, G. (Ed.): *Berufliches Arbeitsprozesswissen. Ein Forschungsgegenstand der Berufsfeldwissenschaften.* Nomos Verlag, Baden-Baden: p. 205-221.

Spöttl, G. (2002): *Developing Curricula for the Training of "K-Workers". A Work Process Oriented Concept for Curriculum Development.* Deutsche Gesellschaft für Technische Zusammenarbeit (GTZ), Universität Flensburg. Flensburg.

Spöttl, G. (2003): *Work Process Analyses as Instrument for Developing Standards.* Report. biat. Kuala Lumpur, Flensburg.

Spöttl, G. (2005): *Sektoranalysen.* In: Rauner, F. (Ed.): *Handbuch Berufsbildungsforschung.* W. Bertelsmann Verlag, Bielefeld: S. 112-117.

Tissot, P. (2004): *Terminology of Vocational Training Policy. A Multilingual Glossary for an Enlarged Europe.* Office for Official Publications of the European Communities, Luxembourg.

Chapter 4: Industry Needs a Flexible and Competent e-Workforce

It should always be the prime orientation for training that it finally has to be "preparation for successful performance at the workplace". Due to increasing complexity and rapid technological advance work itself is undergoing radical change and so is the workplace. Hence, training according to yesterday's parameters can no longer be successful today.

It is extremely important for Malaysia's economy to keep the competitive edge over its neighbouring countries. In order to maintain this cross-national economic advantage the development of most effective training is regarded as a national priority.

The first article in this chapter explains the position of the Federation of Malaysian Manufacturers with regard to necessary aspects of training which need to be addressed in a k-economy. Very much along the lines of what the "The Club of Rome" has described as the need for "anticipatory" and "participatory" thinking, future success at the workplace in industry has to rely heavily on qualifications such as creativity and readiness for lifelong learning which had traditionally not been associated with performance at the workplace.

In the second article the importance of the organisational dimension of training in challenging the requirements of the modern workplace is emphasized. Polytechnics and community colleges are regarded as the upcoming institutions for advanced training, best suited for coping with the requirements of the k-workplace. Hence, institutional reform is regarded as a much needed step in the drive towards upgrading the effectiveness of the public training institutions.

And finally the third article goes beyond national industry onto the level of the multinational companies. It has a clear message: global players need global competence. Indeed the main orientation marks for training are directly related to the effects of globalisation, i.e. competitive prizes and quality products and services. For both these aspects to become realistic targets for the economy a well-trained workforce is a mandatory condition. This has been cast in the term of "People Excellence".

Meeting the Needs of Industry: The Challenge to Training and Education Institutions

Datuk Paul Low Seng Kuan

Introduction

Even with the unemployment rate as low as 3,6 % for 2006 statistics indicate that a high number of our local graduates in Malaysia are reported to be unemployed due to the changing rules and nature of global trade, resource allocations and competition.

Some of the published comments include:

"Universities have a bigger role to play than meeting market needs."

"To cater to specific market demands, we have vocational schools and technical colleges."

"The job market has changed. Now no one works in one place for life."

"Universities are not responsible for manpower planning but rather human resource development."

The above statements, while being very applicable for nation-building, do not give much confidence in preparing for the future. We have a high number of unemployed graduates who need to be retrained to fit into the job market, while without foreign labour our private sector will come to a standstill.

The challenge to training and educational institutes is to develop ways to co-operate, collaborate and consummate programmes that are industry relevant. Nation-building components must also be embedded to create the comprehensively trained worker. To enable this to happen we turn to the industrial perspective of how new models of learning could be incorporated for meeting the needs of industry.

New Models of Learning

Since the beginning of the eighties, especially with the substantial advancement in the field of microelectronics, technology has become the driving force of industrial competitiveness in the global economy. Industrial enterprises have recognised that having the technological know-how and the ability to manage such intellectual assets allows them to determine the rules of competition. They are able to set industrial standards, which other competing firms must follow, and are able to introduce new features or products much earlier than their competing counterparts. Faced with intense competition and constant change in a technology-driven environment, enterprises have realised that people are their most sustainable and strategic asset. Advantages gained from re-engineering exercises, cost cutting, currency depreciation or devaluation, and seeking trade protection are only temporary in nature. But the ability to recruit, develop, and retain a high-performing workforce could provide the intellectual capital to sustain competitive prowess long after the results of these other measures have diminished. To stay competitive, companies cannot have the luxury of lead-time to hire fresh graduates and go through the lengthy training process.

Compounding the challenge of building the workforce to reach a high level of performance is the changing nature of work itself. In the past, under a lesser changing and dynamic environment, technology life spans were longer and hence processes, procedures and practices were more stable and defined. The scope and details of a person's job were defined by well-formulated job specifications that were not subject to frequent changes over time. Today, the situation is different. Constant change is the order of the day. Processes, and hence work, are more interdependent and are subject to change in order to meet the changing requirements of technology, customer requirements, closer collaboration with suppliers and the need to globalise. Flatter, downsized organisations and the convergence of technology mean that the workforce is required to deal with the multi-faceted and multi-dimensional nature of their work, requiring multi-disciplinary skills and perspectives. Graduates often arrive naive to the changing dynamic global industrial environment.

The response to these dramatic changes has been to highlight the importance of training within organisations. Paradoxically, many education and training institutions have been slow to respond to meet these trends resulting in a skills and knowledge deficiency gap that is still in existence even in more industrialised countries. Bridging this gap is not just about producing graduates with the right subject discipline required by industry. Graduates must also have the right attitude, acumen and interpersonal skills to deal with a work environment as described above. Criticism of academia by the industry, for not producing the right types of graduates, mainly concerns this failure to develop traits in students that are suited to the business environment.

Passion for Learning

We are all aware that knowledge has become an important resource to have in any organisation. Most of the skills required by industry are knowledge-based. Particularly in an environment of constant and frequent changes, current knowledge becomes obsolete and is not as relevant as new circumstances come into existence. Moreover, required multi-disciplinary skills mean that the individual must have a working knowledge of other disciplines. Knowledge is the basis of an understanding of the changes that are taking place in an increasingly more complex environment. In turn, this will lead to changes in perception and hence attitude and mind-set. Therefore, having the passion for continuous learning and the skills to acquire new knowledge has now become a generic requirement for any person's employability in industry (see Figure 1).

It may seem ironic, but students coming into the industry underestimate the extent of learning that they will have to do. They lack an appreciation of the importance of knowledge acquisition. One reason could be that in a work environment there is no need to prepare for exams. While institutions of education measure a student's performance from examination results, work organisations measure their performance in relation to the carrying out of jobs at a satisfactory level of efficiency. Perhaps educational institutions should balance student assessments to have both academic and project work that is industry focused.

The key parameters of having the ability to learn continuously are:

- The ability to search for information from raw data and subsequently to use insufficient information to make decisions.

- The ability to use technology to acquire information. The proficient use of computers and the internet is an area which needs to be emphasised.

- The ability to network with people of other disciplines with the view of sharing information. Most models of learning present today do not provide students with the opportunity to have cross-faculty interaction.

- The ability to understand inter-related issues of societal, organisation and business dimensions.

Figure 1: Skills- and Knowledge-Based Work

Skills-based Work	Knowledge Work
Well defined domain of expertise. Job driven	Creation of new solutions and options. Competency driven.
Established skill-sets and well–defined tasks	Dynamic blend of experience, expertise,education, intuition, skills, and competencies applied to unique situations,problems & conditions
Largely observable, explicit, bounded	Invisible,tacit, boundless
Often captured in labour hours, costs,inputs & outputs	Captured in relationship, intellectual capital, roles, experiences

Perception of Quality

In an academic environment there is no concept of "the customer". In business, the existence of a firm rests primarily on its ability to satisfy the customers' needs. This customer orientation requires the enterprise to meet the quality expectations of the customer in terms of performance, reliability and value of the product. In fact, successful enterprises operate business processes and maintain a corporate culture that is highly customer focused. Similar conditions do not exist in the environment of education institutions. Understandably, in most cases the orientation is towards passing examinations, and in passing examinations one is not required to achieve 100 %, but achieve above a threshold usually 50 %. The quest to strive for perfection is missing. The result arising of this is that fresh recruits in industry often lack the will to achieve.

New models of learning should try to instil the drive to achieve, perhaps through the use of teaching methods that encourage competitive spirit to be built-up. Of course, this can be done through extra curricula activities such as sports and games but since not everyone does these activities, some other ways need to be found. Perhaps role-playing exercises in simulated environments need to be introduced.

To give the student a concept of quality and its customer orientation, courses in quality management and marketing could be introduced – especially to technical and engineering courses. At the same time, inherent in most quality management courses are techniques of systematic problem identification, ways to achieve clear thinking, use of analytical tools and finally, finding the right solution.

Creative Thinking

In the age of increased dynamic technological and intensive competition, Malaysian industry has been forced to move up the value-added chain, being involved in more research and development activities. Our ability to do these intellectual activities requires people to be creative.

Institutions need to encourage more creative dissent. There is a need to encourage more tolerance for the expression of different viewpoints and originality of ideas. We should eliminate forms of "negativism" that place undue restrictions, implicitly or explicitly, on individuals when they try to explore and learn. Students should be taught that they are allowed to question assumptions and mind-sets. This could require changes in our perception of social norms. Students should be encouraged to be different if they think it is necessary. They should feel comfortable in more open expressions of their views. A constantly changing environment and the need to add-value to gain competitive advantage demand creativity, lateral thinking, agility and risk taking.

While one would encourage a certain degree of individualism to allow for the flourishing of originality, it is also important to avoid moving to the other extreme of over criticism. A high degree of individualism without the balance of respect for the overall interest could be detrimental and counter productive. Business process integration requires working in teams and in most cases, inter-departmental and inter-disciplinary interactions are required. Therefore, being an effective team player is essential. The new model of learning should ensure that a balance is maintained between the two extremes of overly individualistic behaviour and strict conformance to unitary norms.

Education experts should look into this matter in more depth in order to find out ways to teach these values. Perhaps there is a need for the teaching of creative arts coupled with the existence of an environment in education institutions where these values are allowed to develop. This could also require changes in teaching and coaching methods as well as teacher-student relationships.

To this effect, the Federation of Malaysian Manufacturers (FMM) has initiated a project together with Festo (a manufacturer of electronic equipment), the young design engineer award in the area of manufacturing. The main objective of this competition is to enhance creativity, teamwork and to stimulate projects and products that will be industry relevant. In 2001, a total of 17 projects from our leading institutions took part. For the 2002 competition we have received more than 32 project proposals, including almost all Malaysian institutions of higher learning and training, both public and private sector.

Outward Orientation in Outlook

Malaysia's success in industrialisation has in the past, and will in the future, been closely linked with the world economy. Our growth is linked to export-oriented industries. With the current trend in globalisation, many enterprises will be required to internationalise their operations. This could be in the form of cross-border investments, working with business partners in other countries and using the resources available in any place in the world in order to gain more sustainable competitiveness. The implications arising from these trends are that skills in international management on cross-cultural platforms are becoming a key competency for industrial enterprises.

To cope with these requirements, we cannot afford to have students with an attitude of parochialism and self-centredness. There is no room for inwardness and rigidity in the conduct of business in the international arena.

New models of learning could include:

- The need to encourage cross-cultural interactions with the enrolment of foreign students in local education institutions.
- The need to promote the interest in geography. This will help to give better appreciation of overseas markets and consumers.

Hands-on Working

With flatter organisational structures and the continuing empowerment of employees, especially knowledge-based professionals, employees must have both the agility and capability to do a number of tasks which are not traditionally related to their field of academic study. While the worker develops his core competencies in skills and knowledge, he is required to carry out his job in a manner that is productive and practical. This requires the worker to do his work with a "hands-on" approach. There are often complaints by industry that new graduates fail to appreciate this point. The passivity in this is often displayed by new recruits who seemingly perceive that hands-on work is not within their scope.

To deal with this problem perhaps the conduct of academic studies could include:

- More opportunity to interact with industrial enterprises,
- The use of part-time lecturers from the industry to supplement the full-time academic staff.

Need for Education Facilities to Support Continuous Lifelong Learning

While the above has covered areas relating to the qualitative aspect of the relevancy of education to industry needs, there is a critical need to ensure that there are sufficient facilities to cater for continuous lifelong learning of the working population. This is necessary, not only to upgrade skills and acquire new knowledge, but also to equip the adult workforce with the ability to find jobs between economic sectors. We need to implement the following arrangements, currently lacking in Malaysia:

- A system of part-time study leading to modular accreditation to pursue higher qualifications,

- Increased accessibility of degree courses through industry relevant diploma courses,

- The use of distant learning to support the above since adequate facilities will not be available widely throughout the country,

- Greater accessibility and flexibility for industry to work with institutions.

Conclusion

Malaysia's manufacturing sector has been the engine of growth, especially for the last decade. This sector is today at the crossroad of change. Its ability to sustain growth will depend on its ability to deal with a fast changing environment that is more integrated with the world economy and more technology driven. Industrial enterprises must be able to produce goods at lower costs with better quality, but also must have the innovation and marketing capacity to move along the value-added chain. The key issues for human resource development to meet the needs of industry are not only the acquisition of the necessary skills and expertise, but also the attitudinal and conscious changes in work culture and habits. Concurrently, adaptive skills and high agility are required to deal with the constant changes that are coming from the market and technological advances. New models of learning in education institutions must take these needs into account to be more relevant to the industry.

Educational Strategies for the K-Economy: Laying the Foundation for A Flexible and Competent Workforce[1]

Dato Ahamad bin Sipon

The Knowledge-Based Economy

The publishing of this book is topical in the current education climate given the challenges we face in preparing knowledge workers for the knowledge economy.

This chapter will begin by describing the characteristics of the k-economy and proceed to explain how the education sector can play its role in preparing workers for this new economy. Naturally, where possible, cited examples are based on Malaysian experience.

We begin by taking a look at characteristics of the k-economy. The understanding of these characteristics will benefit everyone with respect to thinking about the preparation of the workforce for the new economy. The Third Outline Perspective Plan of Malaysia describes the knowledge and characteristics of a knowledge-based economy as follows:

- Knowledge is information that is interpreted and used by decision-makers to meet their goals. It is a public good in that there is no additional cost when shared with other users and others cannot be excluded from using it once it is created.

- Knowledge is generally divided into two types, namely, knowledge about technology and knowledge about attributes or tacit knowledge. The latter refers to knowledge gained from experience and is often a source of competitive advantage.

The characteristics of a knowledge-based economy can be described as follows:

- Existence of abundant resources.

Unlike most resources that deplete when used, knowledge input is ever expanding in tandem with technology and innovation.

- No location barrier.

Innovation in technology opens access to resources and markets all over the world, creating virtual market places and organizations. There will be increased mobility of workers and capital. Tuckett (1997) provides a succinct appraisal:

> "In today's world, you can design a product in Milan, borrow the money to produce it in Frankfurt, run it up in Taiwan, market it from Madison Avenue, and buy it everywhere."

- A highly educated labour force.

---

1   The author acknowledges the contributions of Dr.   Mohamed Rashid Bin: Navi Bax and Dr. Mohammad Naim Bin Yaakub in writing this paper.

The knowledge economy produces a better-informed population as the government invests more on human development. Workers contribute to ideas, skills and knowledge by using the latest technology.

- A high level of per capita wealth.

Knowledge-based investments generate increasing returns and therefore, more wealth for all.

- Open cosmopolitan society attractive to global talent.

There will be ample opportunities for local learners to tap foreign knowledge and learn of best business practices. This is as world-class infrastructure will encourage foreign investment. The population will be willing to accept and put into practice new ideas and technologies and hence, local companies will become fit and fully equipped to face global challenges.

- Well connected to other global knowledge nodes.

Connectivity to the rest of the world and technology sharing, as well as technology transformation, will be made easy with the free flow of information with lower cost, and reliable infrastructure encouraging information and technology sharing.

- A shift from top-down hierarchical organizational structures to flatter shared-structures such as networks of semi-autonomous teams.

IT development and communications technology will lead to better interaction among workers. There is active involvement of workers in contributing ideas and decision-making.

- Skills and knowledge are key assets.

Skills and knowledge become the main assets for the economy to gain competitiveness.

- Information and communications technology (ICT) is the pillar of the know-ledge-based economy.

Access to networking is essential in acquiring and disseminating knowledge. The Internet is a key driver of ICT, especially in the development of E-based activities, resulting in new approaches to doing things.

The Role of Public Institutions

The Malaysian Ministry of Education, through its public education and training institutions, has a direct role to play in three of these features i.e. a highly educated labour force, skills and knowledge as key assets, and Information and Communications Technologies (ICTs) as pillars of the knowledge-based economy. Indeed, many educational strategies have been developed by the Ministry of Education, fulfilling the responsibility of preparing a flexible and competent workforce that is IT-savvy. The smart school project is one such example at the school level. This project involves 90 pilot schools. The main project deliverables are the development of electronic courseware, the supply and installation of physical infrastructure and the development of e-learning management systems. Another IT-related project is the Economic Planning Unit Initiative. The objective of this project is to upgrade the computer literacy of teachers and students. It will provide physical infrastructure in the form of computers, IT Labs and software for schools.

At the post-secondary level, efforts have been initiated by agencies who are continuing to implement fully-networked polytechnic campuses with Management Information Systems riding over them. The first polytechnic to be fully networked was Polytechnic Sultan Salahuddin Abdul Aziz Shah in Shah Alam. The campus network provides the infrastructure needed for the deployment of the Total Campus Management System. This system enables administrators and lecturers to perform various administrative, teaching and learning functions both online and electronically. The system includes, among others, a Management Information System, Student Information System, Hostel Management System and Intelligent Timetable Scheduling System. Efforts are under way to train a group of multimedia experts from the polytechnic lecturers to develop multimedia products that can be accessed online by students to increase their understanding of difficult concepts in technical education. Efforts are also under way to provide computer networks and a Management Information System to other polytechnics, enabling e-learning to become a reality for more students.

Technological Change and Competency

With increasing specialization and rapid technological change, the fortune of a nation's economy depends, to a large extent, on a knowledgeable and highly skilled workforce. Rapid technological change requires a flexible and competent workforce that is adaptive to change. This produces new and higher qualification demands on managers, engineers, technicians, supervisors and production operators. To increase a developing country's competitiveness in the era of globalisation and knowledge-based economy, various measures can be implemented aimed at:

- Improving the responsiveness of public training institutes to market demand,

- Expanding the role of the private sector in skills training,

- Strengthening linkages between training and technological and structural change.

In preparing a country for, or sustaining it in the knowledge economy, technical education, especially in the field of information and communications technology, is indispensable. An excellent technical education system can help to propel a country forward and sets the speed and direction of change for the new economy. In this respect, the sub professional layer is of great importance under the current occupational strata. In terms of job title, these sub professionals are usually called engineering assistants, technical assistants, technicians, middle level executives and the like. As we find ourselves getting deeper into the era of globalisation and knowledge economy, a comprehensive curriculum, world-class delivery system and educational infrastructure are essential for the development of flexible and competent sub-professionals.

Institutions that focus on developing these sub-professionals are commonly called polytechnics, technical or technology institutes, and community colleges. In Malaysia for example, the role and central goal of public polytechnics and community colleges is to provide competent, flexible and motivated middle level technical staff and responsible citizens as workforce for the nation, with the possibility of further education and training. For any country, a flexible and competent workforce is a precondition for international competitiveness, increased productivity and the capability to cope with technological and global economical developments. In Malaysia's case, its goal is to become a fully industrialised country and a regional hub of education and excellence in the near future, at the latest by the year 2020. Therefore, it is essential to produce a workforce equipped with professional competence based on the standards and requirements of the global workplace and market. Flexibility, creativity and innovative dynamism are needed to increase the range of courses offered, to introduce new approaches and methods of teaching and learning, to improve management and to have an overall increase in efficiency and quality. Therefore, education and training for the sub-professionals has to be planned and managed using a systemic approach.

Besides the generic fields of technology and engineering, it is of increasing importance in this decade to acquire technical know-how and industry-oriented skills in modern technologies, together with work ethics and high moral values. Lateral thinking, creativity and life-long learning are catalysts of modern professional competence. To develop the innovative and technological capabilities, technical contents have to be combined with competencies in planning, design and communications, methods of problem solving, teamwork and social networking. Extended cooperation and inter-action with industry are necessary to guarantee practice relevance and to match curriculum with market and production needs in a dynamic and fast changing environ-ment. Theory and practice, as well as learning and working, have to be interlinked, and the traditionally separated vocational training and technical education sectors are merging. More and more work systems are incorporating management based on participation, linked to teamwork and quality circles, with promotion based on skill ladders and company support. This marks the breakdown of the division between mental and manual labour. It also demands multi-skilling to create and increase functional flexibility, continuous upgrading and reskilling, formally or informally, internally or externally. The requirements of learning may involve vertical or horizontal integration of knowledge and skills, rendering the distinction between blue and white collar workers blurred (Bhopal et al. 1991).

Polytechnic Education

In its efforts to prepare a sufficient number of young Malaysians to meet these challenges, the Ministry of Education has established a nationwide system of postsecondary education and training, namely public polytechnics and community colleges. As far as polytechnics are concerned, their primary tasks are to:

- Provide broad based industry-oriented technical education and training to upper secondary school-leavers to impart the necessary competencies of
    - technicians and technical assistants in the various fields of engineering,
    - junior- and middle-level executives in the commercial and services sector;

- Provide relevant practice-oriented technological and entrepreneurial education and training to upgrade basic skills and to encourage self-employment;

- Promote collaboration with the private sector through programs such as the Time-Sector Privatisation, Industrial Attachment of Lecturers, Industrial Training of Students as well as research and development programmes.

Malaysian polytechnics have developed specific strategies to ensure that their graduates are competent for the workplace.

Polytechnic education in Malaysia offers a total of 75 courses in the fields of Engineering, Commerce, Hotel and Catering, Graphic and Industrial Design, and Apparel and Fashion Design. To make these courses industry-relevant, their curricula are developed from input by stakeholders through their membership in curriculum advisory committees. These stakeholders are representatives from industry, government and higher learning institutions. Input from these stakeholders is also solicited when designing new courses. Additionally, regional workshops are conducted to gather stakeholders from industry organisations and state government agencies in order to analyse the industrial needs at the regional and local level. Once courses have been identified, their curricula are developed to contain substantial practical components. In designing these practical components, the following issues, as suggested by Praetz (2001), are considered:

- What learners need to know and be able to do.

- What developmental activities will assist their learning.

- What skills and knowledge can be applied routinely in the workplace.

- How the students will integrate and consolidate their learning to ensure that competency is achieved.

- What assessment activities will cumulatively recognise performance at the standard required.

Internal Validation

Any education and training programme must incorporate a feedback loop that will describe the extent to which the programme has achieved its objectives. One such feedback can be obtained from its graduates, through Tracer Studies, which is the real acid test of the programme. In the Malaysian Polytechnics case, tracer studies on polytechnic graduates have generated several findings:

- Polytechnics graduates are satisfied with the curriculum.

- Polytechnic Education can enhance one's career and educational pathway.

- 30 percent of polytechnic graduates pursue further education.

- 85 percent are working in the private sector.

- 85 percent are employed within 4 months of graduating.

- 87 percent say they will repeat their polytechnic education if given the chance.

Findings from the Tracer Studies are being used for continuous improvement of various aspects of polytechnic education in Malaysia. This is a strategy that every education and training institution should adopt to make their programs relevant to customers' needs.

The Professionally Competent Worker

To develop a professionally competent worker, curriculum content for a workforce preparation programme must encompass the knowledge, skills and attitudes of the individual, aside from their technical competence. A professionally competent worker, employers say, is one who is a team player, respectful of others and has good communication skills. Therefore, graduates of any education and training programme must be able to demonstrate professional competence and not just qualifications. A "qualification" is what is written on paper while a "competence" is what is demonstrated by the worker at the workplace. To this effect, students of workforce preparation programs should be required to undergo several months industrial training or other forms of industrial attachments during the course of study to develop workplace knowledge, skills and attitudes, where part of the trainee evaluation is done by industry personnel. Additionally, co-curriculum activities should be offered in areas of uniform organisations such as Red Crescent and Military Cadets, Hobby Clubs and Sports Clubs. Through these activities, students can inculcate all the necessary non-technical skills and attitudes demanded in the current workplace.

References

Bhopal, R. S., Phillimore, P., and Kohli, H. S. (1991). *Inappropriate Use of the Term 'Asian': an Obstacle to Ethnicity and Health Research.* Journal of Public Health, Volume 13, Number 4, p. 244-246.

Praetz , H. (2001). *NOIE Report - NOIE's The Current State of Play.*

Tuckett, A. et al (1997). *The Learning Divide. A Report of the Findings of a UK-wide Survey on Adult Participation in Education and Learning.* National Inst. of Adult Continuing Education, Leicester, England.

Siemens' Strategy for the Transformation of Global Needs into Market Success through the Concept of "People Excellence"

Tan Sri Rainer Althoff

Introduction

The lack of engineers and the necessity of technical education is a widely debated issue of the public not only on a national but also on an international level. Two of the main questions in this discussion are 1. How can this lack be overcome? and 2. What can technical education contribute to solve this problem?[1] Therefore, it is the aim of this article to outline a distinct vision for the future of technical education in a globalised world. This vision is manifested in the appeal to young people and their parents to orientate their vocational choice towards solving the needs which arise from global mega trends such as population growth, demographic change, urbanization or climate change. Young people should concentrate early on attaining technological knowledge at school and they should then qualify for career opportunities offered by companies which challenge our present day demands with social responsibility, technological know-how and cultural sensitivity. These efforts must be encouraged strongly by the governments and, their education systems. Only by doing this, i.e. by. fostering technical education financially, institutionally and culturally, the challenges of the global mega trends can be met. The companies which take on this challenge will be able to compete successfully on the global market.

In order to develop this vision, we must first gain an overview regarding the main global developments and their impact on the economy. Subsequently, with the example of the human resources development at Siemens it will be demonstrated that there is an actual chance to bring this vision into reality. As part of this it will be necessary to define Siemens' corporate principles and the actual economic strategy of Siemens and then to characterize the underlying assumptions and aims of human resource development at the company.

---

1   In order to give a few examples for this problem, cf. http://www.csmonitor.com/2006/0810/p07s02-woeu.html, 23.10.2007, for Germany, cf.
http://www.industryweek.com/ReadArticle.aspx?ArticleID=12139, 23.10.2007, for the oil and gas industry, cf. http://www.azstarnet.com/dailystar/156775, 23.10.2007, for public sector in Arizona, cf. http://www.electronicsweekly.com/Articles/2007/07/12/41796/lack+of+engineers+threatens+uk+economy.htm, 23.10.2007, for the UK, cf.
http://www.bworldonline.com/BW101907/content.php?id=054 , 23.10.2007, for the mining industry. For the role of technical education to overcome the shortage of engineers, cf. e.g. http://imperia5.vdi-online.de/imperia/md/content/presse/48.pdf, 23.10.2007, pp. 3.

Global Outlook

By 2025, the world will have to deal with the consequences of several global developments, which are already taking place now: The earth will be home to nearly eight billion people – two billion more than today – and most of them will be living in cities. In addition, life expectancy is continuously increasing in both the developing and industrial nations. Consequently the world of tomorrow will be shaped in large measure by the mega trends urbanization and demographic change, which will have an unprecedented impact on our lives and on vital sectors of the national economies. Furthermore, these sectors will be simultaneously affected by the consequences of climate change. Under these circumstances, ensuring adequate supplies of energy, water and other everyday necessities while guaranteeing mobility, security, healthcare, industrial production and environmental protection will be a major challenge.[1]

It seems that Siemens – with its cross-sector portfolio, technological leadership and worldwide presence – is much better positioned than most other companies to provide the solutions needed to meet the requirements of tomorrow's world. The company's innovative and future-proof solutions generate competitive advantages for its customers and lay the basis for profitable growth.[2] Therefore, it appears that the company is about to benefit already from getting involved with the global mega trends. By a thorough analysis of future developments Siemens has been able to identify market opportunities related to global mega trends and has been capable to identify key variables, methods and strategies, which enables it to compete successfully in the global market..

One of the factors, of its own success which Siemens identified in a long learning process, is the occupational *capabilities of its employees,* because they are one of the important foundations of the company's *competitive competence.* These capabilities of the employees are actually the key to the future development of the company.

However in a wider perspective, the attitude of competitive competence and human capabilities are also very important for the development of the economy of a nation.. This is in particular true, since the mega trends are already taking shape in the worlds mega cities and have already a noticeable effect on the nations of the world. Therefore, several *challenging questions* regarding the capabilities of the individuals of a nation and of its competitive competence are arising:

- Can all the necessary qualifications in the key industries be made available on time?

---

1   Cf. http://esa.un.org/unpp/p2k0data.asp on population growth, 30.09.2007, on demographic change, e. g. in Germany, 30.09.2007, http://www.weltbevoelkerung.de/pdf/wbb_2007_ zusammenfassung.pdf , 30.09.2007, on urbanization and on climate change, http://www.hm-treasury.gov.uk/independent_reviews/stern_review_economics_climate_change/stern_review_report. cfm, 30.09.2007.

2   Cf. http://www.siemens.de/index.jsp?sdc_p=c61fi102693910mo1382664ps7uz3&sdc_bcpath, 30.09.2007, and the categories "energy", "mobility", "industry", "water", "security" and "health care", which are mentioned and which can be found on this website.

- Are the human resources developed according to the need of the nations economy?

- Do parents and the educational institutions know, how the future will look like in the long run?

- Do parents and the educational institutions appropriately try to attract the children of today to get engaged in research?

- Does the young generation know, what kind of education will pay off later on?

- What kind of knowledge should be generated today?

These questions can only be answered to the effect, that the children, the parents, and the educational institutions of a country must be able *to understand the need of the world and the economies* on the planet for technological solutions. It is also crucial that they understand as well *the impact of the global mega trends on their environment.*

In fact, the world and the economies on the planet will have an extensive demand for electronical engineering, information technology, and naval architecture, because the mega trends will cause serious challenges in these areas. Therefore, as Siemens has already acknowledged, the capabilities of the companies and nations will rely to a high degree on the availability of experts in these fields, i.e. ultimately on an early, constant and exhaustive technological education and training.

This insight is followed immediately by the question regarding the strategy for the establishment of this kind of education and training. Does a working example, which can be taken as an orientation, already exist? How does Siemens develop the qualification of the technical experts today?

Corporate Principles

All efforts of Siemens in the field of technical education and training are embedded in the broader context of the company's corporate principles, of its long term market-strategy and of its strategies in human resources development. The corporate principles and the economic strategy give the basic guidelines for Siemens' economic action and thus for the company's human resources development as well. Consequently human resources development is an integral part of the efforts to achieve the company's strategic aims and the economic strategy intends to implement the company's corporate principles .[3]

The ethical qualities "diversity", "open dialogue", "mutual respect", "clear goals" and "decisive leadership" define Siemens' corporate culture. These corporate principles enable the company's employees to work together in a global network. Thus, Siemens

---

3   For the relation between Siemens corporate identity, its economic strategy and its human resource development cf.
http://www.siemens.com/index.jsp?sdc_rh=null&sdc_flags=null&sdc_sectionid=0&sdc_secnavid=0
&sdc_3dnvlstid=&sdc_countryid=0&sdc_mpid=0&sdc_unitid=999&sdc_conttype=4&sdc_contentid
=1305784&sdc_langid=0&sdc_pnid=&, 03.10.2007.

acknowledges that its employees are the key to its success and *empowers them to achieve excellent performance.*[4]

Figure 1: The Factors which Shape Siemens Corporate Culture

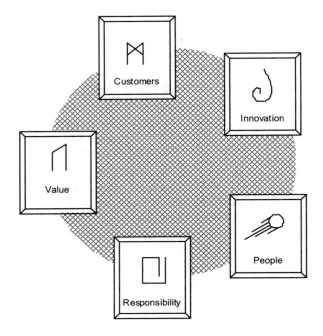

Source: Fit for 2010 (Fit₄2010)

Performance and Portfolio

This focus on the capabilities of the employees is for Siemens the basis for achieving the goals of the programme "Fit₄2010" This is the intermediate-term programme to ensure the company's further development, and i.e. to improve its performance. The general aim of this programme is to ensure that the company will achieve a profitable growth and increase its value. Moreover, the programme wants Siemens to grow at least twice as fast as the global economy in order to be as profitable as its top competitors. In this context, the company is already focusing on promising markets in which it can capture and systematically strengthen leading positions, in order to develop its successful portfolios strategically.[5]

---

4   http://www.siemens.co.th/portal/home/eng/zDoc/Aboutus/SiemensProfileNewEnglish.pdf,   p.8.,
      12.10.2007.
5   Cf. Performance, https://portal.siemens.com, 25.09.2007, on the goals of Fit₄2010 and Fit₄2010,
      https://portal.siemens.com, 25.09.2007, on the role of the human resources development in this
      context. Cf. on this also http://w1.siemens.com/de/corporate-
      responsibility/grundsaetze_und_management/strategie.htm, 12.10.2007.

Strategic Portfolio Development

The portfolio orientation is based on a portfolio development strategy. With it, Siemens intends to occupy leading positions in all the markets, in which the company is already successful, in order to ensure continued profitability in challenging economic situations. To achieve this aim the company applies two methods: Mainly, it is strengthening the businesses of its market-leading Groups through both acquisitions and organic growth. Alongside this, the company endeavours to find strong partners in areas where it does not have the resources to do this on its own.[6]

People Excellence

The Concept

One of the social techniques, which Siemens applies to ensure progress in the development of strategic concepts such as "Fit$_4$2010", is called "People Excellence". The term describes an educational programme, with which the company improves the knowledge and experience of every employee and particularly, promotes the further development of talented people, "who want to do things and are able to assume more responsibilities – in particular young leaders and technical experts", This is achieved by creating "a culture that stimulates everyone to excel".[7]

Consequently "Fit$_4$2010", is a programme which applies "People Excellence", to ensure that the already high performance of Siemens managers will be further improved. It, enhances Siemens' global talent pool, invigorates expert careers and develops a high performance culture.[8]

Therefore, it can be said that the actual task of "People Excellence" is to implement and to promote the idea of high performance throughout Siemens by fulfilling the tasks which lie ahead.

Achieving a High-Performance Culture

Siemens acknowledges that outstanding employees are the key to its success. Only highly motivated individuals enable the company to meet and exceed the expectations of the customers and investors, i.e. to enhance its performance in terms of Fit$_4$2010.

Therefore, it is one of most important tasks of "People Excellence" to create a climate inside the company, which keeps the employees motivated and enables them to unleash their full potential. The necessary cultural basis or culture of work can be described as a *high performance culture* and defined as one *in which employees measure themselves against the best of the best, accept personal responsibility and strive to excel*. It is the

---

6   Cf. Fit$_4$2010, https://portal.siemens.com, 25.09.2007, and http://w1.siemens.com/de/corporate-responsibility/grundsaetze_und_management/strategie .htm, 12.10.2007.

7   The Four Main Action Areas of People Excellence, Siemens AG, 09/25/2007.

8   https://portal.siemens.com, Fit4 2010, 25.09.2007 and http://www.siemens.com/index.jsp?sdc_rh=null&sdc_flags=null&sdc_sectionid=0&sdc_secnavid=0 &sdc_3dnvlstid=&sdc_countryid=0&sdc_mpid=0&sdc_unitid=999&sdc_conttype=4&sdc_contentid =1305784&sdc_langid=0&sdc_pnid=&, 16.10.2007.

function of this culture that the employees become or remain highly qualified and intensely committed and thus providing Siemens with a staff, with which the company can develop and produce world-class products, services and solutions.[9]

In the creation and development of such a work culture the corporate culture itself plays a crucial role: Its values, i.e. "diversity", "open dialogue", "mutual respect", "clear goals" and "decisive leadership" are the guidelines for human resources development. This means *firstly* that the company's human resources staff engages in open dialogue with the other employees concerning their goals, achievements and prospects for further career development (open dialogue, mutual respect). *Secondly*, Siemens creates a working environment in which every employee knows exactly what is expected of him or her. The company's human resources staff provides regular feedback so that the employees are assisted in developing their potential to the fullest. Based on a precise evaluation of individual performance the human resources staff, defines specific career opportunities and determines appropriate compensation for every employee. (diversity, clear goals, decisive leadership). *Thirdly*, Siemens offers its staff excellent career prospects on various levels (mutual respect). In 2006 the company had hired 75,200 employees worldwide, 36 percent of whom were holding university degrees.[10]

Performance Management Process

In order to measure and improve the performance of its employees everywhere throughout the Siemens world as well as in order to promote the development of the high performance culture by "People Excellence", Siemens' human resources development has developed and applies a method called "Performance Management Process". This term describes a *powerful tool for appraising employee performance in terms of carefully defined criteria and nurturing the talented young people who will one day lead the company.* It *enables* Siemens *to evaluate the skills and achievements of individuals* in all its departments, regional companies and corporate units. Once the company has identified the strengths of its top talents and key experts, it can implement the development measures that will best equip these talents to apply their unique expertise and capabilities for the benefit of the company's' customers and investors.[11] Moreover, the company can strongly support those employees, who are not among "the best", "the key players" or the "champions".[12]

---

9   Fit₄More, People Excellence, http://www.siemens.com/index.jsp?sdc_p=i1420432z3ft55mls 3u20o1419476i1419461pGB06cz2&sdc_bcpath=1415713.s_0,&, 16.10.2007.

10 Ibid and The Four Main Action Areas. Cf. note 7.

11 Ibid. For the actual application of this method, cf. Siemens AG (Ed.): Achieve a high performance culture. How we recognize and develop everybody's personal potential? People Excellence. Set standards, 33 (2007), pp. 6.

12 The Four Main Action Areas. Cf. note 7.

Increasing Siemens Global Talent Pool

Siemens' top talents are people who have great potential and who consistently produce outstanding results. These are the future leaders of the company – the individuals who will be responsible for safeguarding the company's future and ensuring that it remains a market leader in all its business areas. In addition to being highly motivated themselves, excellent employees inspire others to produce excellent results. They are willing to make difficult decisions and take personal responsibility for the consequences of their action.[13]

Figure 2: The Qualification level of Siemens Employees

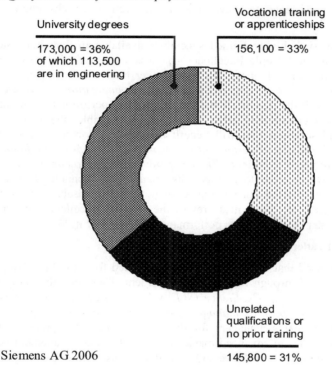

University degrees

173,000 = 36%
of which 113,500
are in engineering

Vocational training
or apprenticeships

156,100 = 33%

Unrelated
qualifications or
no prior training

Siemens AG 2006   145,800 = 31%

The ability of Siemens to recognize and nurture these top talents from early on is a decisive factor in its success with implementing strategic programmes such as Fit$_4$2010. Therefore, the company invests consistently in the "People Excellence"-process for gifted employees by means of an individual development dialog, a structured, extremely ambitious individual development plan and an annual "Top Talent Balance"[14] Furthermore, Siemens' global management team demonstrates a strong personal involvement in cultivating its high potentials. Members of the Managing Board regu-

---

13 Fit4More Cf. note 9.
14 Siemens AG, Achieve a high performance culture, pp. 10.

larly hold interactive Web conferences with the company's top talents, giving participants the opportunity to discuss important company-related issues directly with their executive managers. In addition, Siemens' next-generation leaders from around the world regularly meet personally with the president and chief executive officers.[15]

Improving Career Prospects for Scientists and Engineers

Siemens is a technology leader in many areas and according to Fit$_4$2010 it intends to hold this position in the future. This is essential in today's business environment, where companies that fail to launch new products in time are severely punished. Therefore, it is indispensable for the company to have people employed with the knowledge, dedication and persistence to drive innovation, even when challenging economic situations occur.[16]

In order to have such highly trained specialists available in due time, Siemens has established within the "People Excellence"-process some attractive new career tracks for its top scientists and engineers. In these career tracks, the company's technology experts *can channel all their energy into developing innovations*. They are no longer required to deal with the organizational duties typically performed at the management level. An intense focus on their areas of specialization enables these experts to create the products and solutions that will benefit Siemens' customers. During fiscal year 2006, *Siemens identified and designated key experts at the top- to middle-management levels in promising high-tech fields. The company's aim was to continue expanding the network of experts* in order to maintain its unparalleled technology expertise – the know-how that spawns the outstanding innovations indispensable for success in the global marketplace.[17] By these measures of the "People Excellence" programme, the company is confident to enhance its performance in terms of Fit$_4$2010.

Strengthening Leadership Excellence

Siemens is convinced that first-class results as expected from the Fit$_4$2010 programme can only be achieved through first-class management. Therefore, the company has set up the *Siemens Leadership Excellence (SLE)-scheme* inside the "People Excellence"-process in *order to prepare its managers for the challenges of today and tomorrow*. This programme prepares managers for their future roles very precisely by linking Siemens-specific topics to advanced management methods and leadership skills. Thus, the company is optimistic to achieve and exceed the aims of strategic programmes such as Fit$_4$2010.[18]

In particular, the Siemens Leadership Excellence-scheme (SLE-scheme) enables the company's managers to play a key role in creating a corporate culture that fosters and rewards top performance. Therefore, this programme qualifies them to align leadership and value standards, to share experiences in the company, to impart corporate-wide

---

15 Fit$_4$More Cf. note 9.
16 Ibid.
17 Ibid. For the actual implementation of the career tracks, cf. Siemens AG: Achieve a high performance culture, pp. 13.
18 Fit$_4$More Cf. note 9.

business management tools, to ignite motivation for new approaches, strategies and tools within the company and to facilitate a global, cross business network of management. Moreover, it empowers them to be pioneers of a high performance culture, i.e. role models, who incarnate this kind of culture on a daily basis.[19]

Since the programme was launched in October 2005, more than 80 per cent of Siemens' top executives have attended SLE courses. Worldwide, more than 250 managers have completed the programme, and the feedback from participants has been overwhelmingly positive. SLE is proving to be a key tool for creating and maintaining a high-performance culture at Siemens and thus achieving the objectives of economic strategies which underlie Fit$_4$2010.[20]

Figure 3: Siemens Employees Worldwide

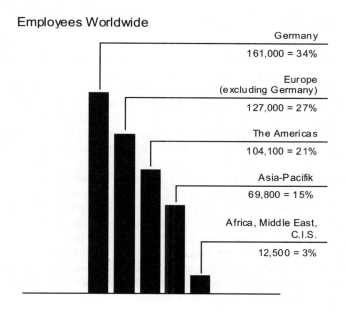

Employees Worldwide

Germany
161,000 = 34%

Europe (excluding Germany)
127,000 = 27%

The Americas
104,100 = 21%

Asia-Pacifik
69,800 = 15%

Africa, Middle East, C.I.S.
12,500 = 3%

Siemens AG 2006

Worldwide vocational training programs

For more than hundred years, Siemens has been intensely involved in providing *vocational training* and *further training* (Lammers 2007, p.6). The actual activities, measures and programmes of this kind are accomplished parallel to the efforts of

---

19 Ibid. For the actual implementation of the career tracks cf. Siemens AG: Achieve a high performance culture, pp. 16.
20 Fit4More Cf. note 9.

establishing a high performance culture within the company and have reached a considerable size, and scope: Today, about 9,600 young people are enrolled in the company's vocational training and work-study programs, including 7,100 from Siemens and 2,500 from other companies. In Germany Siemens offers a comprehensive range of training programs, preparing participants for new types of jobs in information technology, metalworking, electrical engineering and business administration. In addition, the company sponsors special programmes for high school graduates and work-study programmes for university students such as a Bachelor of Engineering in electronics and information technology, engine construction, mechatronics and the like. During the fiscal year 2006, the company has spent € 291 Mio. for education, vocational training and further training. Therefore, Siemens is one of the largest education and training providers of Europe. On a global level, Siemens spent € 463 Mio. for education and vocational training of young employees as well as for further training. This sum is bound to rise, because in the same year Siemens employed 14,100 more staff than the year before, i.e. in total 474,900 employees worldwide.[21]

Furthermore, Siemens is exporting its *dual work-study system*, which combines theory and practice, to many of its Regional Companies around the world. Outside Germany, about 4,200 young people are currently enrolled in Siemens *apprenticeship programmes*, which have been adapted to country-specific requirements. With the *Siemens Mechatronic Systems Certification Programme*, for instance, the "*Siemens Technik Akademie Berlin*", the company's technical academy, provides training in cooperation with educational institutions in other countries such as *Nanjing College of Information Technology* in China. Siemens also provides training for *Mechatronic Systems Assistants, Associates and Professionals,* who – by their "Handlungskompetenz" (acting competency) – are able according to their level of training to act fast, efficiently, independently, responsibly in large-scale systems even in difficult situations (Lammers 2007, p.11). Another example for the company's human resources policy is the *International Employee Development Year*, in which the technical academy trains skilled employees on an engineer level for the tightly focused service in foreign Operating Companies (OC) in order to enable them to process orders and to transfer know how between Siemens-Headquarters and the Operating Companies abroad (Lammers 2007, p.2). This creates an international network, which contributes to the high quality of the company's products and services.[26]

All employees of Siemens enjoy the advantages of being offered, thorough and highly sophisticated technical education and corresponding further training. Within the context of the company's high performance culture , these employees – and therefore Siemens as well – are very well prepared for the technological and economic challenges lying ahead.

---

21 Ibid and cf. Siemens AG (Ed.): Siemens bildet aus. Overview for 2006 regarding all occupations for which the company offers training programmes in Germany, the number of participants, who took part in those programmes, and the costs which, the company has invested in vocational training in 2006.

Summary

With the elements of the "People Excellence"-process, with the emerging high performance culture and with the successful vocational training programmes Siemens has in place a comprehensive education and training system. This system is based on the thorough analysis of the training demands arising from global mega trends. By developing the capabilities of its employees within this system, Siemens has improved its competitive competence and the company can be confident to meet the future technological and economic challenges arising from the global mega trends successfully.

References

Documents:

Lammers, W. (2007): *Technical Staff Development for Operating Companies in Cooperation with Siemens Technik Akademie Berlin*, PowerPoint presentation. Berlin, 07/2007.

Lammers; W.; Webb, D. (2007): *Siemens Mechatronic Systems Certification Programme*, PowerPoint presentation. 10/2007.

Siemens AG (Ed.) (2007): *Achieve a high performance culture. How we recognize and develop everybody's personal potential? People Excellence. Set standards.* 33/2007.

Siemens AG (Ed.) (2006): *Siemens bildet aus. Übersicht über unser bundesweites Angebot.* 2006.

Internet pages:

http://esa.un.org/unpp/p2k0data.asp, 30.09.2007.

https://portal.siemens.com. 25.09.2007.

http://www.azstarnet.com/dailystar/156775, 23.10.2007.

http://www.bworldonline.com/BW101907/content.php?id=054, 23.10.2007.

http://www.csmonitor.com/2006/0810/p07s02-woeu.html, 14.10.2007.

http://www.electronicsweekly.com/Articles/2007/07/12/41796/lack+of+engineers+threatens+uk+economy.htm, 23.10.2007.

http://www.hm-treasury.gov.uk/independent_reviews/stern_review_economics_climate_change/stern_review_report.cfm, 30.09.2007.

http://imperia5.vdi-online.de/imperia/md/content/presse/48.pdf, 23.10.2007.

http://www.industryweek.com/ReadArticle.aspx?ArticleID=12139, 23.10.2007.

http://www.siemens.com/index.jsp?sdc_p=i1420432z3ft55mls3u20o1419476i1419461pGB06cz2&sdc_bcpath=1415713.s_0,&, 16.10.2007.

http://www.siemens.com/index.jsp?sdc_rh=null&sdc_flags=null&sdc_sectionid=0&sdc_secnavid=0&sdc_3dnvlstid=&sdc_countryid=0&sdc_mpid=0&sdc_unitid=999&sdc_conttype=4&sdc_contentid=1305784&sdc_langid=0&sdc_pnid=&, 03.10.2007.

http://www.siemens.co.th/portal/home/eng/zDoc/Aboutus/SiemensProfileNewEnglish.pdf12.10.2007.

http://w1.siemens.com/de/corporate-responsibility/grundsaetze_und_management/strategie.htm, 12.10.2007.

http://www.weltbevoelkerung.de/pdf/wbb_2007_zusammenfassung.pdf , 30.09.2007.

Summary

With the concept of the "Probabi..." explained process, influences the very high work number, points and will its conclusion...

References

Deutsche ...

Chapter 5: Educational Strategies for the K-Economy: Quo Vadis?

This last chapter obviously draws a line from the knowledge economy via an effective system for the training of k-workers to educational strategies on the micro level. When it comes to the learning or instructional process, it is not sufficient to rely on a single strategy. The professionally competent worker must have a multidimensional qualification on the basis of appropriate curricular contents and methods of learning and instruction. Such a unified approach has to safeguard the acquisition of the required knowledge, the skills and the attitudes to cope with changing requirements at the workplace. Hence, in order to attain this qualification educational strategies must focus on the specific requirements of performing successfully at a k-workplace. The educational strategies should target these various requirements in a supplementary way. And finally beyond mastering the work-requirements it must be the target of these strategies to assist in co-shaping a humane-oriented civil society.

The first author has taken the task of defining generic skills necessary for coping in the k-economy, by identifying key generic skills which are essential for learning today and finally by reflecting on different ways of integrating these skills into the TEVT curriculum. On the way from describing an effective system of training k-workers towards actually securing the expected outcomes of training these considerations for the micro level of training are indispensable.

The basis for experimenting with innovative approaches of training lies in the flexibility and versatility which the Malaysian system of training provides. With four ministries involved in training there is quite some duplication, but there also is a degree of differentiation which is unknown in other countries. This differentiation serves as an ideal platform for the emergence of innovative approaches in training. The second author has presented a precise description of this scenario of Malaysia's highly differentiated system of training.

Emerging Generic Skills & Challenges of Learning Systems: Training K-Workers

Shyamal Majumdar

Introduction

In today's global economy driven by knowledge, the foremost wealth of a firm is its human capital or knowledge assets. The Organisation for Economic Co-operation and Development estimates that already more than half the wealth of advanced industrial societies is derived from knowledge capital. The knowledge-based economy recognizes the key role of information-based technologies in providing a basis for the generation, management and utilization of knowledge as never before, and for the emergence of knowledge-based industries. Drucker (1998) predicted that the typical large business enterprise in twenty years from now will have half the number of people in management. Specialists brought together as a cross-functional team will do most of the work. The employment pattern will shift from manual and clerical workers to knowledge workers. Nonaka (1998) believes that one sure source of lasting competitive advantage for business organisations will be knowledge. Successful companies will be those that consistently create new knowledge, are able to disseminate it widely throughout the organisation, and quickly embody it in the new technologies and products. Knowledge-creating organisations invent new knowledge as a way of behaving or being. In this case everyone in the organisation is a knowledge worker (cf. OECD 2005).

The common features of the knowledge-based industries are that they are: inter-disciplinary, oriented towards research and development, information intensive, dynamic and require human capital with high reasoning and cognitive skills.

Organisations are adopting flatter hierarchies, leaner and more flexible in response to change. Strategic alliances among organisations have become commonplace, giving rise to a new phenomenon – the boundaryless organisation. Ashkenas, et al (2002) explained that the boundaryless or virtual organisation is a living continuum, not a fixed state. It is capable of evolving and growing so that the location of boundaries may shift. The levels of the organisational hierarchy may decrease, functions may merge and partnership with suppliers and customers may evolve, thus shifting boundaries to "who does what" to "who knows what" and "who is connected to whom".

The emerging workplace described above demands a set of new generic skills for maintaining employability. In addition to job-specific technical competencies, there is a requirement for a set of generic skills, which are common to a cluster of occupations in order to perform competently as knowledge worker. Specific occupational skills are augmented to growing cognitive skills. These skills are essential for effective parti-cipation in the emerging patterns of work and work organizations. In this chapter the author suggests a list of generic skills for emerging knowledge economy and puts forward the idea of integrating generic skills in the TVET curriculum. In the opinion of the author the successful implementation of integrating generic skills in TVET curriculum will largely depend on the pedagogical, technical and managerial skills of TVET system. TVET systems need to gear up for this mission.

Identification of Generic Skills

A number of research works have been undertaken on generic skills. Examples are the Mayer Committee set up by the Australian Education Council and Ministers of Vocational Education, Employment and Training in Australia (1991), the Secretary's Commission on Achieving Necessary Skills (SCANS) in the United States (1992), the British National Skills Task Force etc. This allows the comparison of generic skills identified in countries like Australia, Britain, United States and New Zealand (see Table 1).

Table 1: Comparison of Generic Competencies

Australia	United Kingdom	United States	New Zealand
Key competencies	**Core skills**	**Workplace know-how**	**Essential skills**
Collecting, analysing and organising information	Communication	Information Foundation skills: basic skills	Information skills
Communicating ideas and information	Communicating Personal skills: Improving own learning and performance	Resources Foundation skills: basic skills	Communication skills
Planning and organising activities	Personal skills: Improving own learning and performance	Resources Foundation skills: personal qualities	Self-management skills Work and study skills
Working with others and in teams	Personal skills: working with others	Interpersonal skills	Social skills Work and study skills
Using mathematical ideas and techniques	Numeric: application of numbers	Foundation skills: basic skills	Numeric skills
Solving problems	Problem-solving	Foundation skills: thinking	Problem-solving and decision-making skills
Using technology	Information technology	Technology Systems	Information skills Communication skills

Source: Moy, J. The Impact of Generic Competencies on Workplace Performance 1999.

Moy's work on key competencies attempted to provide a definition for each of the seven key competencies which can be helpful in understanding generic skills vis-à-vis job-specific skills (see Table 2).

Table 2: Key Competency Definitions

Collecting, analysing and organising information	The capacity to locate information, process and sort information in order to select what is required and present it in a useful way; and to evaluate both the information itself and the sources and methods used to obtain it
Communicating ideas and information	The capacity to communicate effectively with others using the range of spoken, written, graphic and other non-verbal means of expression
Planning and organising activities	The capacity to plan and organise one's own work activities, including making good use of time and resources, sorting out priorities and monitoring one's own performance
Working with others and in teams	The capacity to interact effectively with other people both on a one-to-one basis and in groups, including understanding and responding to the needs of a client and working as a member of a team to achieve a shared goal
Using mathematical ideas and techniques	The capacity to use mathematical ideas, such as numbers and space, and techniques such as estimation and approximation, for practical purposes
Solving problems	The capacity to apply problem-solving strategies in purposeful ways, both in situations where the problem and the desired solution are clearly evident and in situations requiring critical thinking and a creative approach to achieve an outcome
Using technology	The capacity to apply technology, combining the physical and sensory skills needed to operate equipment with an understanding of scientific and technological principles needed to explore and adapt systems

Source: Moy, P. The Impact of Generic Competencies on Workplace Performance 1999.

Generic skills can be structured into a developmental framework. Kearns (2001) offers a model for clustering the generic skills which include the cognitive cluster; interpersonal cluster; enterprise, innovation and creativity cluster; and work readiness and work habits cluster. Figure 1 presents the details of the four clusters of key generic skills required by the 21st century.

Figure 1: Clusters of Key Generic Skills

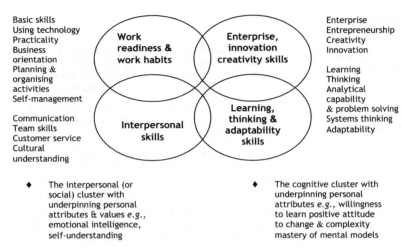

Another model for generic skills is the new competency model which was developed for the United Nations. Kearns describes the model as a broad approach to generic skills that links core competencies and core values with management competencies which are necessary to give impetus to the generic skills in a high performance workplace. It can be seen from the model that commitment to continuous learning is one of the core competencies (see Figure 2).

Figure 2: United Nations Competency Model

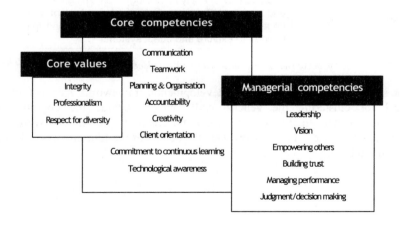

Proposed Generic Skills

Careful analysis of the above reports and working in the TVET (Technical Vocational Education and Training) system for more than two decades leads the author to suggest the following core generic skills for the survival of knowledge workers in the competitive knowledge economy.

- Critical Thinking and Problem Solving Skills:

Knowledge workers need to develop critical thinking skills to define problems in complex, overlapping, ill-defined domains; use available tools and expertise for searching, formulating the problem, analyzing, interpreting, categorizing ideas and finding alternatives; and choosing the best solution.

- Creative Thinking Skills:

Knowledge workers need to develop creative thinking to generate new ideas for solving problems, discovering new principles and new processes and products. Diagnostic and design skills will play an important role.

- Information Handling Skills:

Knowledge workers need to develop the capacity to acquire, locate, search and find information for effective decision making. They need to evaluate the information and know how to use and communicate with it.

- Communication Skills:

Knowledge workers need to develop communication skills in a variety of media for diverse audiences using variety of modern tools particularly Internet communications.

- Teamwork Skills:

Knowledge workers require teamwork for solving complex problems, creating complex tools, services, and products. Collaboration, coordination and teamwork will be the key for success.

- Technology Application Skills:

The capacity to apply technology, particularly computing technology, with physical and sensory skills is essential in the knowledge age. Knowledge workers need to operate equipment with the understanding of scientific and technological principles needed to explore, acquire, adapt and operate systems.

- Autonomous Learning Skills:

Rapid technological changes require the ability to diagnose and prescribe one's own training needs. Knowledge workers will have to manage their own career paths and their own continuous learning of new skills. Learning to learn & life long learning will be the key parameters of survival in this era.

- Cross-cultural Understanding Skills:

In the era of globalization, knowledge workers will have to work in multi-cultural society. They need to have cross-cultural understanding for effective teamwork.

Integrating Generic Skills in TVET Curriculum

There could be differences in the nature and details of generic skills that need to be included in the TVET curriculum among countries in the context of different development stages, policies and priorities. There can be no disagreements about integrating higher order generic skills in the TVET curriculum on priority basis. The integration of essential generic skills into the TVET curriculum will require substantial change, including those that relate to new learning technologies, flexible learning strategies and assessment practices.

There could be many models adopted for incorporating "Generic Skills" components into the curriculum, but two specific models have been very much talked about in this field. The first model is known as "Diffusion Model" whereas the second model is known as "Infusion Model". The essential features of these two models are discussed below.

Diffusion Model

In this model the generic thinking issues arising from different disciplines of education are diffused i.e. taken out from their respective areas and pooled into a common generic discipline or subject known as "Curriculum on Thinking Skills" (see Figure 3).

Figure 3: Diffusion Model

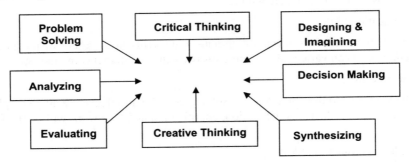

Hence, the implementation of this model in TVET may lead to separate courses on Generic Thinking Skills. These courses being interdisciplinary necessitates the interaction between a wide range of people trained in different fields of knowledge (disciplines) each with its own concepts, methods, body of knowledge and language tackling a common problem from various viewpoints. The interaction may range from simple communication of ideas to mutual integration or organization of the concepts, methodology, procedures, epistemology, terminology and development of generic thinking skills and techniques.

Infusion Model

In this model, the concepts of thinking skills are injected into the various conventional disciplines and subjects without introducing new subjects e.g. thinking education (see Figure 4).

The main issue with this approach is that thinking cuts across the full range of subjects and should be integrated into all. Integration of thinking skills in a subject area is generally difficult to design and implement. It means therefore that teachers of different subject areas and from different levels must be in regular dialogue with each other to validate and confirm whether or not the generic skills are still attuned with the times and disciplines.

However, in the opinion of the author the best way to integrate generic skills in the TVET curriculum is by combining both models through the Hybrid approach. We need to offer both the separate discipline on generic skills as well as integration in different subject contents depending on the requirement of the TVET curriculum.

Figure 4: Infusion Model

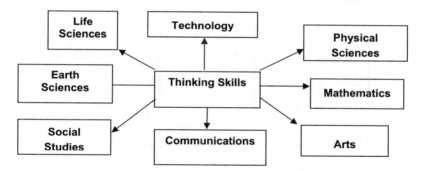

Pedagogical Challenges for Learning Systems

There should be a paradigm shift in educational practice of teaching and learning in knowledge society. The author argues that while learning through facts, repetition and practice, rules and procedures was more adaptive in earlier days, now learning through projects and problems, inquiry and design, discovery and invention, creativity and diversity, action and reflection is more fitting for the present times. So there is a need to develop a conceptual framework on the pedagogical dimensions of learning systems in the knowledge society.

For this purpose, a shift is required in each of the pedagogical dimensions presented below (Table 3). There is an urgent need to recognize the pedagogical shift from a conventional job specific curriculum to a thinking curriculum, from instructive to constructive, from behavioural to cognitive, from didactic to facilitative, from content to learning to learn, from surface learning to deep learning, and from a learner centred approach to a learning team centred approach. The following shift in pedagogical dimensions is tabulated below:

Table 3:   *Shift in Pedagogical Dimensions*

Dimensions	Undesirable	Desirable
Pedagogical Base	Instructive	Constructive
Learning Focus	Content	Learning to Learn
Learning Strategies	Interactive	Collaborative& Interactive
Learning Goal	External Controlled	Autonomous
Learning Theory	Behavioural	Cognitive
Teacher Role	Didactic	Facilitative
Delivery Modes	Fixed	Open
Learning Approaches	Surface	Deep
Learning Structures	Rigid	Flexible/ Modular
Instructional Models	Instructor Centred	Learning Team Centred
Learning Objectives	Information Transfer	Mental Model Change
Learning Methods	Passive	Active

In the opinion of the author, the successful implementation of integrating generic skills in the TVET curriculum will largely depend on the potential for upgrading the pedagogical, technical and managerial skills within the TVET system. TVET systems need to gear up for this mission.

References

Ashkenas, R. et al. (2002). *The Boundaryless Organization.* Jossey-Bass Publication, USA.

Drucker, P. (1998). *The Coming of the New Organization.* Knowledge Management, USA: Harvard Business School Press.

Kearns, P. (2004). *Education Research in the Knowledge Society: Key Trends in Europe and North America.* Australia: NCVER.

Kearns, P. (2001). *Generic Skills for the New Economy.* Australia: NCVER.

Majumdar, S. (2001). *On-line Collaborative Learning.* Proceedings of the Career and Technical Education Annual Convention & IVETA at New Orleans, USA: p 13-16.

Mayer Committee. (1992). *Putting General Education to Work: The Key Competencies Report.* AEC/MOVEET, Melbourne, 1992.

Moy, J. (1999). *The Impact of Generic Competencies on Workplace Performance.* NCVER, Australia.

Nonaka, I. (1998). *The Knowledge-Creating Organization.* Knowledge Management, Harvard School Press, USA.

OECD (2005). *Education at a Glance.* Paris.

Secretary's Commission on Achieving Necessary Skills (1991). *What Work Requires of Schools.* US Department of Labour, (ED 332 054). Washington, DC.

A Historical Account of Skills Training in Malaysia

Pang Chau Leong

A Historical Account of Skills Training in Malaysia

Introduction

In the context of Malaysia's education and training system, "skills training" is not as well-discussed as "vocational training" or "vocational education and training (VET)". In the past, skills training has often been used synonymous with vocational training, or subsumed within the wider notion of VET. It was only over recent decades that the term "skills training" has become an increasingly recognisable component in the country's education and training system, rather than merely been regarded as part of the national education system at large, or VET system in specific.

This paper is an attempt to embark on a journey into, and explore, the early beginnings of skills training and development in Malaysia. In essence, it seeks to scrutinize skills training in the country from a historical perspective. This exploration of the development of the Malaysian skills training system necessarily begins by tracing the development of the country's VET system. The journey ends with a cursory examination of the structure and shape of skills training in the country today, and then having a glimpse of new developments taking place.

Early Developments of Vocational Education and Training (VET) in Malaysia

The idea of providing for VET (in reality, trade skills training) in Malaysia could be traced back to the late 1890s. Francis Wong & Ee (1975, p. 157) noted that in 1897, there were already discussions on setting up trade schools to prepare Malay boys to work as mechanics and fitters on the railways. However, in practice, much of the early initiatives catered mainly for traditional arts and crafts, as seen in 1900 when the government of Selangor engaged several local craftsmen (a wood-carver, a silversmith, a blacksmith and a tailor) to teach their crafts to Malay students residing in the Malay Settlement on the outskirts of Kuala Lumpur (Philip Loh, 1975, p. 110-111). In 1902, similar craft training was organised in the neighbouring state of Perak, with the establishment of a school named "Malayan Art School" under the patronage of its Sultan, providing training for weaving, embroidery, wood-carving, silversmith's work, pottery and mat-making (ibid, p. 111).

The British colonial government of Malaya was first seen to get involved in VET when it appointed a Commission in 1902 to look into vocational education (Ahmad 2003, p. 4). In 1906, a school known as the Teacher Technical School was established by the Public Works Department of the Federated Malay States to train technical assistants for the Railways and Public Works Department (Maznah 2001, p. 30). However, the school was closed at the start of the First World War but reopened in

1918. Using English as the medium of instruction, it conducted apprenticeship courses to serve the needs of several public departments including the Public Works Department, the Federated Malay States Railways and the Survey Department (Ahmad, 2003, p. 4; Philip Loh 1975, p. 111). Upon completion of training, successful apprentices were employed as "clerks of works", surveyors or draftsmen. In 1919, the government set up a committee to review the needs for technical and industrial education and it put forward various recommendations concerning training in the country, including the call for an expansion of technical training in terms of language used and industry sectors covered. The measures are summarized and paraphrased from Philip Loh (1975, p. 111):-

• Establishing trade schools using Malay as the medium of instruction;

• Building a new technical school using English as the language of instruction;

• Establishing an agricultural school;

• Providing training facilities for the Forest department; and

• Providing better salaries for technically trained employees in government departments to bring them in line with the clerical service.

The next significant development was the opening of a Federal Trade School in Kuala Lumpur in 1926 to provide full-time three-year courses to train mechanics, fitters, machine workers and other technicians (Ahmad 2003, p. 4; Philip Loh 1975, p. 111). The school then had a small student capacity of fifteen to twenty per year and primarily served the needs of the Public Works Department. The Education Department took over the school in 1931 which by then was called Technical School, to serve the needs of other public departments apart from the Public Works Department, as well as business enterprises such as mines, estates and private firms (Ahmad 2003, p. 5; Philip Loh 1975, p. 112). Later, it also took in private students leading towards Technological Certificates awarded by the City and Guilds Institute of London. Later, three other trade schools were built in Penang, Ipoh and Singapore (part of Malaya at that time) to prepare apprentices as artisans in trades such as mechanics, plumbers, fitters, electricians and blacksmiths. These developments clearly marked the expansion of institutionalized vocational training in Malaya which were geared to meet the needs of the country's industry. It is unclear from the literature as to the actual extent to which the expansion had taken place. It was noted, however, by Maznah (2001, p. 30) that the pioneer technical school was renamed Technical College in 1945, which was then upgraded in 1972 to Universiti Teknologi Malaysia, a full-fledged university.

In 1955, two years before Malaya actually gained her independence from the British colonial government in 1957, the Malayan Alliance Government took over office. In the same year, it set up an Education Committee headed by Abdul Razak Hussein, the Malayan Education Minister, to review the existing education system and to formulate an education system for post-independence Malaya (Pang 2005, p. 3). The study led to a report in 1956 – known as the *Razak Report* – which recommended a unified education system for all Malayans. Eddy Lee (1972, p. 16) suggested that this Report promoted the policy of establishing a vocational stream alongside the general secondary school system. This view was strongly reflected from the Report's recommendation that technical education and training be organized into three levels, namely technical colleges, technical institutes and trade schools which were elaborated on as in Table 1 (ibid, p. 4; Ahmad 2003, p. 5; Francis Wong & Ee, 1975, p. 158-159).

Table 1: Levels of Technical Education and Training,Razak Report 1955.

Type of Institutions	Description and Functions
1. Technical Colleges	Institutions of post-secondary education to provide full-time courses for those who had completed a full (five years) secondary education.
2. Technical Institutes	Institutions of post-lower secondary education – to provide courses of three-years duration for those who had completed three years of secondary education, and who seek employment as technicians.
3. Trade Schools	Schools, especially in rural areas – to provide two-years courses for those who had completed a primary school education; courses should be related to the environment of the school and the needs of employment, and normally conducted in the Malay language.

Source: Paraphrased and tabulated from Francis Wong & Ee 1975

Many other developments took place, changing further the character and shape of the country's VET system. In 1960, another report widely known as the *Rahman Talib Report* was published, recommending more changes to the technical and vocational school system (Eddy Lee 1972, p. 16). The Report noted that there were only eight rural trade schools in 1960, with a student enrolment of 616 only. It proposed that the majority (up to 70 per cent) of pupils be given the opportunity in "post-primary" schools to acquire manual skills whilst preparing for the Lower Certificate of Education exami-nations, that is at the end of three years of secondary education. Eddy Lee (1972, p. 16) observed that the proposal to incorporate vocational subjects in lower secondary schools did not take off because of the shortage of vocationally-qualified teachers. Instead, specialized vocational education was made available at the upper secondary level after 1965, albeit on a very small scale as seen from student enrolment figures. For example, in 1969 the total enrolment in vocational and technical schools was 3,786 compared with the total secondary school enrolment of 468,816 (ibid). The Rahman Talib Report is particularly significant for the country's VET system because it brought about the segregation of the formal secondary school system into academic and vocational streams (MOE 2007). Under the report, junior technical (trade) schools were converted to secondary trade school which, in turn, were converted in 1968 to secondary vocational schools (SVSs). Even up to the present day, the SVSs conduct trade courses which are of two-years duration, mainly in the engineering field

In 1979, another high-powered Cabinet Committee headed by the Deputy Prime Minister at that time, Dr. Mahathir Mohamed, was formed to study the implementation of the national education policy, including to review the country's technical education and vocational training system (Pang 2005, p. 4). The ensuing *Cabinet Report of 1979* reaffirmed that the country's upper secondary education should comprise of both the academic and vocational streams (MOE 2007).

Shaping of the Malaysian Skills Training System

Based on a review of historical developments in the field of VET in Malaysia, from the 1956 Razak report up to the Cabinet Report of 1979 described above, Ahmad (2003, p. 6) observed that the Malaysian VET system had progressively assumed a distinct structure, which was dominated by three different streams or pathways, distinguishable in terms of producing the country's workforce, namely: (1) higher education; (2) technical and vocational education; and (3) skills training (Table 2). This observation highlighted that by the late 1970s, skills training had already emerged as a component of Malaysia's education and training system. Ahmad (2003) also noted that the structure suffered from a lack of coordination whereby the polytechnics, community colleges, as well as technical and vocational schools came under the purview of the Ministry of Education, whilst skills training institutions came under other Federal Ministries (ibid, p. 6). In justifying his investigation into the coordinating role of the National Vocational Training Council (NVTC), he argued that "the key to ensure the system works effectively" lies in the existence of an efficient and influential coordinating body such as the NVTC (ibid, p. 31).

Table 2: Main Streams of the Education and Training System in Malaysia.

Stream or Pathway	Institutions	Workforce Preparation
1. **Higher education**	Universities and other institutions of higher learning, both public and private	Professional and managerial personnel such as engineers, architects, and surveyors
2. **Technical and vocational education**	Polytechnics, technical colleges and (more recently) community colleges	Supervisory personnel such as technical assistants and supervisors
3. **Vocational skills training**	Skills training institutions, public and private	Skilled and semi-skilled workers

Source: Paraphrased and tabulated from Ahmad 2003

A similar description of the Malaysian education and training system in which skills training was a major component was later made by Rashid & Nasir (2003, p. 5-6), who highlighted that the mainstream secondary school system comprised of three different pathways. One was a pathway that led to higher education (thus, called the "academic" pathway), whilst VET was segregated into two distinct streams namely the technical and vocational education stream, as well as the skills training stream. They basically distinguished between the three pathways as follows:

(a) Tertiary or higher education in universities and other higher educational institutions;

(b) *Technical and vocational education* undertaken largely in the formal school system under the Ministry of Education; and

(c) Post-secondary technical and vocational education and training (including skills training) undertaken through the *skills stream* of the secondary vocational schools but predominantly by public and private skills training institutions.

In contrast to the above-mentioned accounts of the Malaysian VET system, several other studies highlighted that *skills training based on National Occupational Skills Standards (NOSS)* had become a significant component of the national VET system. The *"Basic Study on Designing a Dual training Scheme in Malaysia"* undertaken from 1997 to 1999 by a large team of German consultants described the Malaysian VET system in a detailed manner, namely in terms of a structure that was made up of three subsystems, excluding tertiary and higher education (Blumenstein et al. 1999, p. 43-48). It distinguished technical and vocational training undertaken by the Ministry of Education (1st subsystem) from training under the purview of other Ministries (2nd subsystem). In addition, it isolated and highlighted the National Occupational Skills Standards and Certification System as the third component of the Malaysian VET system (3rd subsystem). The subsystems were elaborated as follows:

1st subsystem: Comprised of *technical education and vocational training* undertaken in schools at the upper secondary level under the purview of the *Ministry of Education (MOE)*. It was therefore completely integrated into the general education system, leading to the Malaysian Certificate of Education (Sijil Pelajaran Malaysia, SPM) as the leaving qualification. Holders of the SPM qualification had a choice of several educational or vocational avenues such as:-

• Higher education in colleges or universities offering degree courses;

• Courses in polytechnics, technical colleges or agricultural colleges offering diploma / higher national diploma qualifications;

• Teacher training;

• Various skills training programmes conducted outside the Ministry of Education (referring to 2nd subsystem); and

• Direct entry into the employment market

2nd subsystem: Comprised of *technical and vocational training* which did not come under the purview of the MOE, but were administered by *other Federal Ministries* such as the Ministry of Human Resources (MOHR), Ministry of Youth and Sports (MYS), and Ministry of Entrepreneurial Development (through its agency MARA) as well as private training institutions. The training institutions could be classified according to the level of occupational skill standards and the certification system, based on the National Occupational Skills

Standards (NOSS). The qualifications involved were mainly the Malaysian Skills Certificate Levels 1-3, diploma for Level 4, and advanced diploma/degree for Level 5.

3rd subsystem: The standardisation and certification of occupational skills based on the *National Occupational Skills Standards and Certification* **System**. It started with a three-level skill certification system (basic, intermediate and advanced) but in 1992, a new 5-level skills qualification framework was introduced, followed by the adoption of an accreditation approach in 1993. The accreditation of training centres and their training courses was conducted by the NVTC.

Another study known as the *"Strategic Review of Technical Education and Skills Training (TEST) in Malaysia"* was undertaken by Australian consultants as part of an Asian Development Bank technical assistance project, during the same period as the above-mentioned "Basic Study" (DEETYA 1998, p. 1). In assessing the position of TEST in Malaysia during the 1998-1999 period, the study confirmed that vocational education under the purview of the MOE was one major component of the Malaysian public sector VET system. It also found that training conducted by the MOHR, MYS and MARA using NOSS as a basis, formed the other major component of the national system.

A more recent attempt at describing the structure of the technical education and vocational training system (TVET) system in Malaysia was made in 2005 for a study undertaken on behalf of the *World Bank*. Pillay (2005) categorised Malaysia's TVET system into five main pillars which are briefly outlined below:-

1st pillar: Public higher education system which caters mainly to SPM school-leavers, that is those who do not take up pre-university studies. It excludes universities and university colleges, but includes polytechnics and community colleges under the Ministry of Higher Education, technical schools under the Ministry of Education as well as training institutions under the Ministry of Human Resources, Ministry of Entrepreneurial Development and Ministry of Youth & Sports (p. 7-8).

2nd pillar: Malaysian Skills Qualifications Framework, a five-tiered skills certification system based on the NOSS which was introduced by the National Vocational Training Council in 1993 (p. 8).

3rd pillar: Company-based training, which comes under the Human Resource Development Fund established in 1993 to promote the training of employees (p.9).

4th pillar: Private higher education, largely under the purview of the Private Higher Education Institutions Act 1996, and accredited by the National Accreditation Board (p. 9).

5th pillar: Continuing education and training which caters to the demands of employers, community or society at large for further education, skills upgrading, retraining, career advancement and enrichment.

All the above descriptions of the structure of the VET system in Malaysia by numerous researchers and commentators serve to emphasize that skills training has increasingly made its presence felt since the 1970s, but it was only after the early 1990s that it became entrenched in the country's education and training system. The growing significance of skills training has been seen to coincide with the introduction of NOSS-based training in the early 1990s.

Legislations Concerning Skills Training.

The development of skills training in Malaysia can also be examined in the context of the country's education and training legislations. During the mid-1990s, the country engaged in massive legislative educational reforms, in part as a response to the rapid growth of private higher education in Malaysia (Tan 2002, p. 3). Consequently, five pieces of legislation were enacted and they have remained in force even up to today. The main federal legislation regulating the education system in Malaysia is the *Education Act 1996 (Act 550)* which takes a very broad view of education that clearly encompasses all forms of training including skills, specialised, job-based and continuing training. This can be seen from subsection 35(2) of the Act which stipulates that "technical education" includes the provision of:

a) Skills training;

b) Specialised training related to a specific job;

c) Training for the upgrading of existing skills; and

d) Such other technical or vocational training as may be approved by the Minister of Education. (Malaysia 1996a, p. 26)

Another piece of related legislation, the *Private Higher Educational Institution Act (Act 555)* which has been enacted to specifically regulate private higher educational institutions in Malaysia, also adopts the same broad view of education. The Act 555 adopts several interpretations which show its intent to treat training as a component of education, albeit higher education, in Malaysia. As examples, the following terms are widely used in the Act:

"Course of study" describes a training programme. (Malaysia 1996b, p. 11).

"Higher education" means "instruction or training on or teaching of a course of study leading to the award of a certificate, diploma or degree upon the successful completion thereof." (ibid, p. 12).

"Student" means a person receiving education, instruction, training or teaching from or in a private higher educational institution. (Malaysia 1996d, p. 13)

The third piece of major legislation, the *National Accreditation Board Act 1996 (Act 556)*, confirms that the architects of educational reforms during the 1990s regard training as merely a part of education in Malaysia. The Act 556 emphasises that a course of study may include any training programme (Malaysia 1996c, p. 6), an interpretation which is similarly adopted in Act 555.

Therefore from the standpoint of the Malaysian legislative framework, up to the 1990s and going into the new millennium, skills training had always been part of and subsumed within education at large, including higher education. It was only in the last few years that skills training began to assume a more distinctive entity in relation to education in the country's legislative framework. In particular, skills training has been given a more prominent position in the country's education and training system through two pieces of recently enacted legislations. The legislations are:

(1) The *Skills Development Fund Act 2004 (Act 640)* which was officially gazetted on 31 December 2004 (Malaysia 2006a, p. 2), thus establishing the Skills Development Corporation to manage the Skills Development Fund. The Fund has been established to grant skills training loans to trainees of approved skills training programmes, especially those based on NOSS (ibid, p. 14).

(2) The *National Skills Development Act 2006 (Act 652)* came into effect on 1 September 2006 after it was officially gazetted on 29 June 2006, with the following mandate:-

> An Act to promote, through skills training, the development and improvement of a person's abilities, which are needed for vocation; and to provide for other matters connected therewith. (Malaysia 2006b, p. 7)

The Act 652 is perhaps the most significant development because for the first time in the history of skills training in Malaysia, a national legislation has been enacted solely and exclusively for skills training and development. In addition, the meaning and scope of 'skills training' has been clarified and more importantly, given a statutory interpretation which can be used to distinguish it from other components of the country's national education and training system. The Act defines "skills training" as:

> "...work based and industry oriented activities which aim to provide the knowledge, skills and attitude required for effective and efficient performance of a task or job, and includes refresher, further, updating and specialized job-related training." (ibid, p. 8).

The Act provides for the establishment, review, variation and use of National Occupational Skills Standards (NOSS), which till then has never been covered in any national legislation. Thus, it can be said that NOSS has finally "come of age" after about thirteen years (that is, since 1973) of existence in Malaysia – that it has finally been given a statutory standing and position in the country's education and training system. The Act 652 also provides for the implementation of a Malaysian Skills Certification System, leading to the award of five levels of national skills qualification, namely Malaysian Skills Certificate Level 1, 2 and 3; Malaysian Skills Diploma; and Malaysian Skills Advanced Diploma. These provisions collectively represent a "watershed" in the development of skills training in Malaysia because in essence, a legislatively-backed skills pathway has been provided for within the country's national qualification framework. This development is expected to give fresh impetus to the skilled workforce development and the promotion of skills-based careers in Malaysia.

Introduction and Provisioning of Skills Training Based on NOSS

The term *"National Occupational Skills Standards (NOSS)"* was first introduced following the decision of the National Vocational Training Council (NVTC) at its No. 4/92 meeting on December 9, 1992 to agree to several measures that sought to improve the national vocational training and certification system in Malaysia (MLVK,

1992, p. 21; MLVK 1993, p. vi-vii). The decision led to the implementation of two major policy thrusts: The first, was to adopt the accreditation approach in the implementation of the national skills certification system; and the second, was to enhance the competency-based training approach in the country's training system. Consequently, a new framework and methodology was adopted for developing the skills standards which would provide the basis for accreditation. These standards became known as "NOSS".

The notion of occupational skills standards in Malaysia, however, can be traced much further back. The idea to establish some form of standards to support trade testing and apprenticeship training in Malaysia went as far back as 1969. With the assistance of an International Labour Organisation (ILO) expert on teaching technique, a Trade Instructors Training Programme was undertaken in 1968 during which 72 instructors were trained. The programme was expanded with the signing of a Plan of Operation agreement between the Malaysian Government and the United Nation Development Programme in June 1969 to include, amongst others, establishing trade skill tests and "the strengthening of apprenticeship standards" (UNDP) (MOLM 1973, p. 45). However, it was not until 1972 that the development of occupational skills standards – known as *"trade standards"* at that time – received greater attention from the government. In early 1972 the Central Trade Standards and Testing Committee (CTSTC) was established, consisting of 10 members of whom 2 represented employers' organisations and another 2 represented employees' organisations (MOLM 1974, p. 79). The tripartite composition of the committee was indicative of the ILO expert's influence at that time. As its name suggests, the CTSTC was charged with the responsibility of developing trade standards and testing for the country at large for the first time. This was affirmed by the expressed functions of the CTSTC which included the following:

(a) To determine the trades for which testing is to be carried out for purposes of common certification; and

(b) To establish, apply and review standards for certification at various levels of performance. (ibid, p.79)

The establishment of the CTSTC, accompanied by the formation of seven ad hoc trade standards committees in 1972 quickly bore fruits in terms of trade standards development. By the end of the same year, *National Trade Standards* for the Basic, Intermediate and Advanced grades had been approved by the CTSTC for three trade skills areas, namely Motor Vehicle Mechanic, Refrigeration and Air-conditioning Mechanic; and Earth-moving Equipment and Constructional Machinery Mechanic (ibid, p. 79). These standards represented the earliest form of occupational skills standards established in Malaysia at the national-level.

Over the years, the development of occupational skills standards in Malaysia experienced many more changes until it reached a major milestone with the enactment of the National Skills Development Act 2006 on June 29, 2006 (Malaysia 2006b, p. 2). Under the new Act, for the first time ever, NOSS development in the country has been provided for by the country's legislative framework. The Act contains provisions specifically for the establishment of NOSS (Section 20), its review and variation

(Section 21) as well as the use of NOSS for curriculum development, assessment and certification (Section 22) (ibid, p. 16-17).

In Malaysia, skills training based on NOSS is today offered by a wide variety of public and private training institutions. As of May 2007, a total of 1,151 different training institutions have been accredited to offer 6,575 training programmes based on NOSS, of which 363 centers are administered by public agencies and authorities, whilst the remaining 788 are privately run (Thomas 2007, p. 19). Within the public sector, 26 accredited centers (478 accredited programmes) come under the Ministry of Human Resources; 165 centers (744 programmes) under the Ministry of Entrepreneur and Cooperative Development; 15 centers (322 programmes) under the Ministry of Youth and Sports; 66 centers (366 programmes) under the Ministry of Education; 10 centers (31 programmes) under the Ministry of Agriculture and Agro-based Industries; 16 centers (55 programmes) under the Ministry of Home Affairs; 15 centers (158 programmes) under the Ministry of Defence; 2 centers (25 programmes) under the Ministry of Rural and Regional Development; 4 centers (8 programmes) under the Ministry of Family, Women and Community Development; 1 centre (2 programmes) under the Ministry of Plantation Industries and Commodities; 42 centers (460 programmes) under various state authorities. In the private sector, skills training is provided by a multitude of training institutions that are operated by employers, associations, companies or enterprises.

Changing Demands: Introduction of the National Dual Training System (NDTS)

Rapid changes in technology and increasing complexity of work processes in Malaysian industries have created new demands on the skilled workforce, namely for knowledge-workers or "k-workers". Realising that the training for k-workers must utilize the workplace as the prime learning environment, the Government of Malaysia decided on 19 May 2004 to implement the *National Dual Training System (NDTS)* commencing in 2005 to produce 31,500 skilled workers by 2010 (MLVK 2005a).

The NDTS has evolved from the Dual Training System Project (DSP) which was formulated with the purpose of strengthening technical education and vocational training in Malaysia by incorporating the dual training system practiced in Germany (DSP 2001, p. 7). The DSP started with a study known as "Basic Study on the Design of a Dual Vocational Training Scheme in Malaysia", undertaken by German consultants during 1997-1999 (Blumenstein et al. 1999). The NDTS involves a two-year training programme carried out at two learning environments, namely 70-80 percent in workplaces and the remaining 20-30 percent in selected training institutions. In terms of training delivery, self-reliant learning, action-oriented teaching as well as learn and work assignments (LWA) have been adopted as the fundamental teaching and learning approaches (MLVK 2005). The notion of "training occupations" was also introduced for the first time in Malaysia to designate the training programmes to be selected for NDTS implementation. With regard to curriculum design and development, a new training document known as the National Occupational Core Curriculum (NOCC) was introduced as the basis for training and assessment (ibid). The NOCC is a new form of training documentation and it differs from training resources used in the existing NOSS-based training because its development has been premised on a work-process orientation.

Some Final Words

The introduction of the NDTS marks another important milestone in the development of skills training in Malaysia. It has been touted as a new national training initiative which has an "extra edge" over the existing NOSS-based training system in Malaysia by virtue of its focus on the development of k-workers, its application of new delivery and methodological approaches such as the NOCC and LWA, as well as its adoption of work process orientation (Hoepfner & Koch 2004; MLVK 2005; Spöttl 2004). Nevertheless, the emergence and development of the NDTS as another component of the national training system, alongside the existing NOSS-based training system has become a source of concern to training providers, employers and other stakeholders. Many have raised reservations on their training outcomes, qualification being awarded, delivery and operational aspects as well as policy implications. Others, however, have regarded the NDTS as the timely successor for the present NOSS-based training system which they think can no longer cope with today's rapid technological change.

In the light of such concerns, it is vital that the respective roles and positions of both the NOSS-based training system and NDTS in meeting the country's skilled workforce requirements are clarified. It is also crucial that the future direction of the NOSS-based training system in relation to the newly-introduced NDTS is determined. Answers as to whether the NOSS-based training system is fundamentally any different from the NDTS should be obtained. Analysis can then be made to ascertain whether the NOSS-based training system should remain as a separate entity from NDTS, or be subsumed, or even supplanted entirely, by the NDTS. Clearly, deep and comprehensive insights are required before leaders and policy-makers are able to make informed decisions on shaping the future direction of skills training in Malaysia.

References

Ahmad, O. (2003). *The role of the National Vocational Training Council in the management of vocational training in Malaysia: A critical evaluation*. Batu Pahat: KUiTTHO

Blumenstein, G., Borgel, H., Greinert, W., Grunwald, E., Jarck, K. & Kaloo, U. (1999). *Basic study on the design of a dual vocational training scheme in Malaysia*. Deutsche Gesellschaft fur Technische Zusammenarbeit (GTZ). Final report, May 1999.

DEETYA International Services. (1998). *Strategic review of technical education and skills training in Malaysia: Strategic options paper - the management and coordination of technical education and skills training (TEST) in Malaysia*. Kuala Lumpur: Economic Planning Unit & Asian Development Bank.

DSP. (2001). *The Dual System Project: Think dual – go dual in training. Getting Malaysia ready for the K-economy*. Kuala Lumpur: DSP, Malaysia / GTZ, Germany.

Eddy Lee (1972). *Educational planning in West Malaysia*. Kuala Lumpur: Oxford University Press.

Francis Wong H.K. & Ee T.H. (1975). *Education in Malaysia, 2nd. Ed.* Hong Kong: Heinemann Educational Books (Asia) Ltd.

Hoepfner, H.D., & Koch, H. (2004a). *Self-reliant learning in technical education and vocational training (TEVT)*. Kuala Lumpur: Dual System Project, Malaysia/GTZ, Germany.

Malaysia, G. o. (1996a). *Education Act 1996 (Act 550)*. Kuala Lumpur: Ministry of Education, Malaysia.

Malaysia, G. o. (1996b). *Private Higher Educational Institution Act 1996 (Act 555)*. Kuala Lumpur: Ministry of Education, Malaysia.

Malaysia, G. o. (1996c). *National Accreditation Board Act 1996 (Act 556)*. Kuala Lumpur: Ministry of Education, Malaysia.

Malaysia, G. o. (2006a). *Skills Development Fund 2004 (Act 640)*. Kuala Lumpur: Percetakan Nasional Malaysia Berhad.

Malaysia, G. o. (2006b). *National Skills Development Act 2006 (Act 652)*. Kuala Lumpur: Percetakan Nasional Malaysia Berhad.

Maznah M. (2001). *Adult and continuing education in Malaysia*. Hamburg: UNESCO Institute for Education / Kuala Lumpur: Universiti Putra Malaysia Press.

MLVK (1992). *Laporan programme "attachment" di agensi-agensi persijilan di United Kingdom untuk mempelajari sistem "accreditation"*. [Report of the attachment programme at certification agencies in United Kingdom for examining the accreditation system]. Kuala Lumpur: Majlis Latihan Vokasional Kebangsaan (MLVK), Malaysia.

MLVK. (1993). *Panduan pelaksanaan Persijilan Kemahiran Malaysia melalui sistem pentauliahan (Edisi pertama)*. [Guidelines for the implementation of Malaysian Skill Certification through the accreditation system. (1st ed)]. Kuala Lumpur: MLVK.

MLVK. (2005). Implementation of the National Dual Training System – guides and rules. (2nd ed.). Putrajaya: MLVK.

Ministry of Education [MOE] (2007). *The National Education System in Malaysia*. Retrieved 2 February 2007, from www.moe.gov.my

Ministry of Labour and Manpower [MOLM] (1973). *Annual report of the Ministry of Labour and Manpower for the year 1970*. Kuala Lumpur: National Printing Department, Malaysia.

MOLM (1974). *Annual report of the Ministry of Labour and Manpower for the year 1972*. Kuala Lumpur: National Printing Department, Malaysia.

Pang, V. (2005). *Curriculum evaluation: An application in a smart school curriculum implementation*. Kota Kinabalu: Universiti Malaysia Sabah.

Philip Loh F.S. (1975). *Seeds of separatism: educational policy in Malaysia, 1874-1940*. Singapore: Oxford University Press.

Pillay, G. F. (2005). *Technical & vocational education (TVET) systems of selected East Asian countries: Malaysia*. Washington, D.C.: The World Bank.

Rashid & Nasir (2003). *Lifelong learning in Malaysia*. Paper presented at the International Policy Seminar, 24-26 June, Seoul, Korea.

Spöttl, Georg. (2004). *Work process orientation of the TEVT system and consequences for NOSS – an instrument for the development of occupational profiles*. Report for Berufsbildungsinstitut Arbeit und Technik (biat), Universitat Flensburg, Germany.

Tan A.M. (2002). *Malaysian private higher education: Globalization, privatization, transformation and marketplaces*. London: ASEAN Academic Press.

Thomas, G. (2007). *Consolidating TVET: Building excellent & productive human capital*. Paper presented at the National technical & Vocational Education & Training Conference 2007, 3 May, Kuala Lumpur, Malaysia.

The Authors

Tan Sri Rainer Althoff

Tan Sri Rainer Althoff is currently the President and CEO of Siemens Malaysia Sdn Bhd and also the Siemens spokesperson for all Siemens operations and affiliate companies in Malaysia. His experience in the field of electrical engineering spans more than 25 years and he holds a graduate degree in Electronics and Electrical Engineering from the University of Wuppertal/ Düsseldorf. Tan Sri Rainer Althoff has spent most of his working life with Siemens AG, first as an engineer for the planning of transportation systems, then in various other positions including as head of export sales in alarm and security systems and as head of mobile networks worldwide. In 1999 he assumed his current position. In 2003, Tan Sri Rainer Althoff was awarded the Federal Service Cross ("Bundesverdienstkreuz") by the President of the Federal Republic of Germany and in 2007 the Darjah Kebesaran Panglima Setia Mahkota by His Majesty, the Yang di-Pertuan Agong of Malaysia. Tan Sri has a keen interest in promoting the social responsibility of private sector companies.

Matthias Becker
Prof. Dr.

Junior Professor for the Vocational Specialisation Metal Technology/ System Technology at the Berufsbildungsinstitut Arbeit und Technik – biat – of the University of Flensburg/ Germany. Becker has published a number of booklets and articles. He holds an Engineering Degree from Cologne University for Applied Sciences as well as a degree in Teacher Training for Technical Education and Vocational Training of the University of Bremen. He is also an automotive mechanic.

Abdul Hakim Juri
Prof. Dr.

Abdul Hakim Juri holds a PhD in Mechanical Engineering from the University of Leeds. He started his career in 1988 as a lecturer in the Faculty of Engineering, Universiti of Malaya and later moved into the local automotive component manufacturing industry. His venture into Technical and Vocational Education started when he was appointed Deputy Director of the German Malaysian Institute (GMI), Kuala Lumpur in 1992. Abdul Hakim Juri became Director of GMI in 1996 and lead the institute for six years until September 2002. During his tenure at GMI, he initiated a preparatory programme to prepare Malaysian students to qualify for study at German Universities of Applied Sciences. In appreciation of his contribution to strengthening bi-lateral relations between Germany and Malaysia, Dr Juri was conferred with the "Bundesverdienstkreuz", Federal Cross of Merits, in March 2003. Abdul Hakim Juri is currently President of Universiti Kuala Lumpur.

Datuk Paul Low Seng Kuan

Datuk Low is the former President of the Federation of Malaysian Manufacturers (FMM). He has more than 30 years experience in business and has served international organizations such as WTO, APEC, ASEM and ASEAN-CCI in various positions. He is a member of the National Economic Actions Council (NEAC), the National Information Technology Council (NITC) and the Industrial Coordinating Council. At present he is the President of the Malaysian Automotive Components Parts Manufacturers Association (MACPMA). By profession Datuk Low is a management accountant and he is a member of the Malaysian Institute of Accountants and the Malaysian Association of Certified Accountants.

Gert Loose,
Prof. Dr.

Gert Loose is the Head of the Occupational Standards and Skill Testing Project on behalf of the German Agency for Technical Cooperation (GTZ) and Adviser to H.E. The Minister of Manpower, Sultanate of Oman. Before coming to Oman he headed the Dual System-Project for the Economic Planning Unit, Department of the Prime Minister in Malaysia and he has continuously served the German-Malaysian Institute, GMI. Gert Loose's past experience includes work with UNDP (Sri Lanka), the World Bank (Kyrgyzstan) and as a programme director for the UNESCO Institute for Education. He also served as the General Adviser to the Governor of the General Organization for Technical Education and Vocational Training (GOTEVT) in Saudi Arabia. He is an automotive mechanic by profession.

Shyamal Majumdar
Prof. Dr.

Shyamal Majumdar is Quality Management Representative (QMR) and member of the governing board of the Colombo Plan Staff College for Technician Education (CPSC). Prior to joining CPSC he served as head of the Computer Science and Engineering Department, Technical Teacher's Training Institute, Calcutta, India. He was also Deputy Manager of the Computer Department in one of the leading banks of India. Shyamal Majumdar has acted as staff consultant for the Asian Development Bank and he is a panel member of the UNESCO Distance Education Workshop. His expertise ranges from information technology and communication to open and flexible learning and multimedia computing.

Steven K. Miller

Steven K. Miller is the former Secretary of the UN Secretary-General's Youth Employment Network. He has worked at both policy and operational levels within the UN system for 23 years. Steven K. Miller began his career in the International Labour Organisation (ILO) in 1982 as Chief Technical Adviser of a project on labour-intensive infrastructure development in Burkina Faso. His expertise focuses on promoting policies and field-level practical applications of labour-intensive infrastructure development in areas such as employment-intensive investment policies, urban employment and remuneration policies. Steven K. Miller holds degrees from Yale College and Boston University.

Pang Chau Leong

Pang Chau Leong currently holds the position of Deputy Director-General at the Department of Skills Development, Ministry of Human Resources, Malaysia. He has accumulated over 25 years of experience in skilled workforce development encompassing competency standards development, curriculum design and development, skills testing and certification, as well as human resource planning. Pang Chau Leong was the pioneer and mastermind of the development of the Malaysian National Occupational Skill Standards (NOSS) and has later on been one of the core developers of the National Dual Training System (NDTS). He obtained his Bachelor of Engineering from the University of Malaysia, and his Masters of Science (Human Resource Development) from the University of Manchester in UK. His current research interest is on comprehensive aspects of the development of the national skills training system in Malaysia.

Yussoff Md. Sahir

Yusoff Md. Sahir is the Managing Director of the German-Malaysian Institute (GMI) in Kuala Lumpur. He has served GMI in various positions since 1993. Yusoff Sahir was involved in many initiatives regarding innovative approaches in TEVT in Malaysia. He received his B.Sc. in Electronic Engineering from South West State University, Minnesota, USA and his M. Edu. in TEVT from University Teknologi Malaysia. Yusoff Md. Sahir continues to serve the development of the Malaysian National Occupational Core Curricula with research and development activities. At present he is preparing GMI for its transition to a new campus in 2008.

Hermann W. Schmidt
Prof. Dr.

Hermann W. Schmidt is the former President of the Federal Institute for Vocational Training (BIBB) in Germany. He presently serves as a member of various international associations such as the Academy of Education, Moscow, the Advisory Board of the European Training Foundation (ETF), the Board of the National Center on Education and the Economy (NCEE), Washington D.C. and the Board of the Center for Research in Innovation and the Society (CRIS), Santa Barbara, USA. Hermann Schmidt is at present a Professor at Duisburg University, Germany and he serves as international consultant for human resource development.

Dato' Ahamad bin Sipon
Dr.

Dato Ahamad bin Sipon is Deputy Director General (Technical Education) in the Ministry of Education, Malaysia. He has served some 30 years in various positions in the field of technical education and vocational training, including his work as principal of two polytechnics, as director of the Polytechnic Management Division and as Selangor State Education Director. Dato Ahamad bin Sipon's international experience includes membership of the board of the South East Asian Ministers of Education Organization Regional Training Center and the advisory panel of the Colombo Plan

Staff College in Manila. He holds a B.E. degree in Electrical Engineering from the University of Adelaide and M.S. and Ph.D degrees from Virginia Polytechnic Institute and State University in the USA.

Andy Smith
Prof. Dr.

Andy Smith is Professor of Human Resource Management and Head of the School of Management at Charles Sturt University, NSW, Australia. Formerly he was General Manager for Research and Evaluation at the Australian National Center for Vocational Education Research and foundation director of the Group for Research in Employment and Training (GREAT). He is an expert in enterprise training and has conducted studies on organizational innovation in workplace training, new management practices and enterprise training and supply and demand for skills in an innovative economy (for the Victorian Department of Education).

Georg Spöttl M.A.
Prof. Dr.

Georg Spöttl is Director and Head of the Institute of Technology and Education (ITB) at the University of Bremen. Formerly he was Founder and Director of the Institute Work and Technology (biat) at the University of Flensburg. He has worked on technical cooperation projects for Saudi Arabia, Yemen, Kuwait, Jamaica, Thailand, Malaysia, and Oman. His expertise ranges from curriculum development and vocational research to qualification research, research in high-tech training, vocational education planning and didactics. He is the author of numerous publications in these areas and has also published in the fields of automotive engineering and CNC-technology. Georg Spöttl has been involved in many projects funded by the European Community. By profession he is an automotive mechanic.

Zanifa Md. Zain

Zanifa Md. Zain is the Director of the Human Resource Section, Economic Planning Unit (EPU), Prime Minister's Department, Malaysia. She is a senior member of the Malaysian Civil Service with 27 years of service in various government agencies. She was involved in various long-term strategic programmes for upgrading the effectiveness of the Malaysian workforce and has been in charge of the human resource section of the development plans which were designed by EPU. Ms. Zanifa Md. Zain holds a Bachelor of Arts (Economics) from the University of Malaya and a Master of Arts in Public Administration from Pennsylvania State University in the USA.

Berufliche Bildung in Forschung, Schule und Arbeitswelt
Vocational Education and Training: Research and Practice

Herausgegeben von Georg Spöttl und Falk Howe

Band 1 Gert Loose / Georg Spöttl / Yusoff Md. Sahir (eds.): "Re-Engineering" Dual Training – The Malaysian Experience. 2008.

www.peterlang.de

György Széll / Carl-Heinrich Bösling / Ute Széll (eds.)

Education, Labour & Science
Perspectives for the 21st Century

Frankfurt am Main, Berlin, Bern, Bruxelles, New York, Oxford, Wien, 2008.
607 pp., num. tab. and graph.
Labour, Education & Society.
Edited by György Széll, Heinz Sünker, Anne Inga Hilsen and
Francesco Garibaldo. Vol. 10
ISBN 978-3-631-56793-7 · pb. € 58.–*

This book presents a selection of presentations during the Fifth Congress of
the International Network "Regional and Local Development of Work and
Labour". The congress took place at the University of Osnabrück in September
2006. However, it was not a traditional congress, but it revived the practice
of "future workshops", which were invented by Robert Jungk. The book
assembles 33 articles covering all social sciences by authors from 16 different
countries: Austria, Brazil, Denmark, Germany, France, India, Italy, Japan, The
Netherlands, Nigeria, Norway, Poland, Russia, South Africa, Spain, and Sweden.
It is dedicated to the democratization of the different spheres of society from
a grassroot-perspective.

Contents: Education · Science · Labour · Peace

Frankfurt am Main · Berlin · Bern · Bruxelles · New York · Oxford · Wien
Distribution: Verlag Peter Lang AG
Moosstr. 1, CH-2542 Pieterlen
Telefax 0041 (0) 32 / 376 17 27

*The €-price includes German tax rate
Prices are subject to change without notice
Homepage http://www.peterlang.de